I0709585

Cofounders: Taj Forer and Michael Itkoff
Creative Director: Ursula Damm
Copy Editor: Gabrielle Fastman

© 2022 Daylight Community Arts Foundation

Photographs © 2021 by Ed Hotchkiss

Afterword © 2021 by Lawrence Weschler

ISBN: 978-1-954119-09-3

Printed by Ofset Yapimevi, Turkey

Daylight Books
E-mail: info@daylightbooks.org
Web: www.daylightbooks.org

Daylight

STATION TO STATION
Exploring the New York City Subway

Ed Hotchkiss

The great thing about the subway, at least for a photographer, is its inhabitants all sitting in that photo shoot called the 2 train, or the N train.

Sometimes I was troubled that I had invaded their private moments with my camera. Often, I wished I could tell my subjects how striking they were, how beautiful, how interesting to be with.

But I couldn't do that. I couldn't have people reacting to me when what I wished to capture were their authentic reactions to their subway experience.

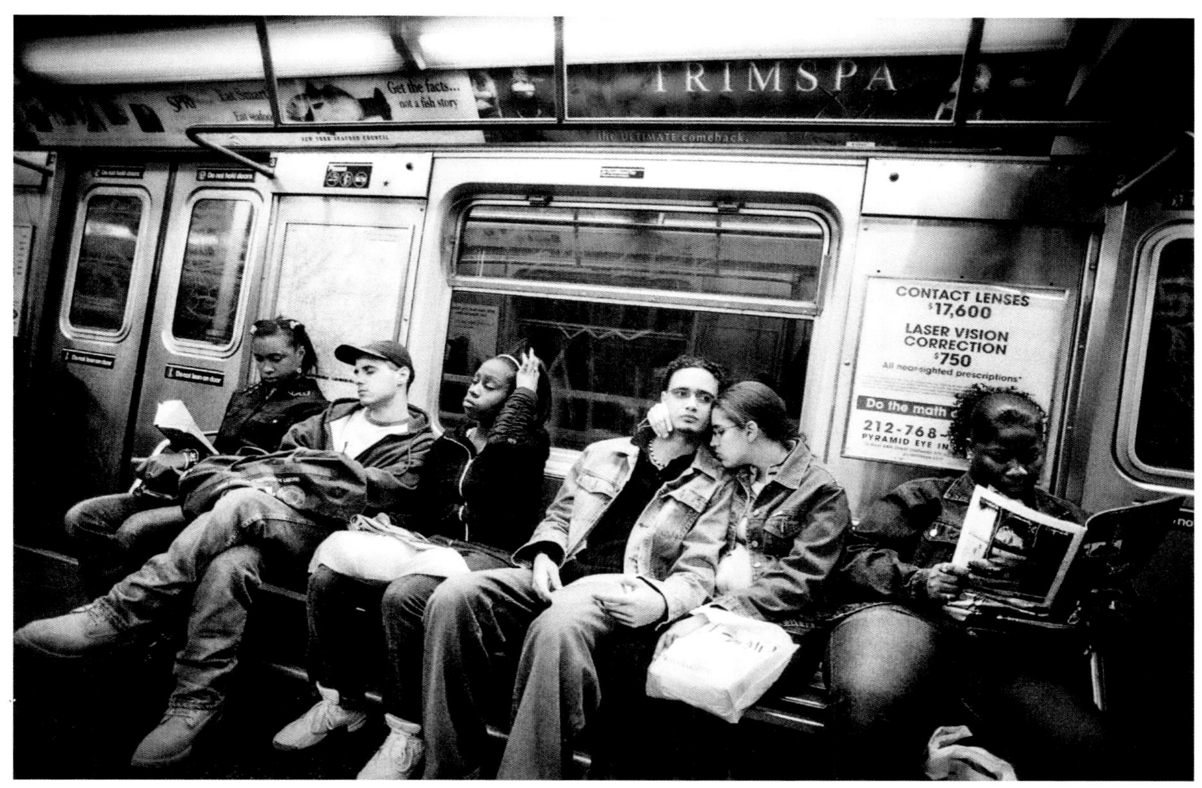
TRIMSPA
the ULTIMATE comeback.
Get the facts...
not a fish story
CONTACT LENSES
$17,600
LASER VISION
CORRECTION
$750
All near-sighted prescriptions*
Do the math
212-768-
PYRAMID EYE

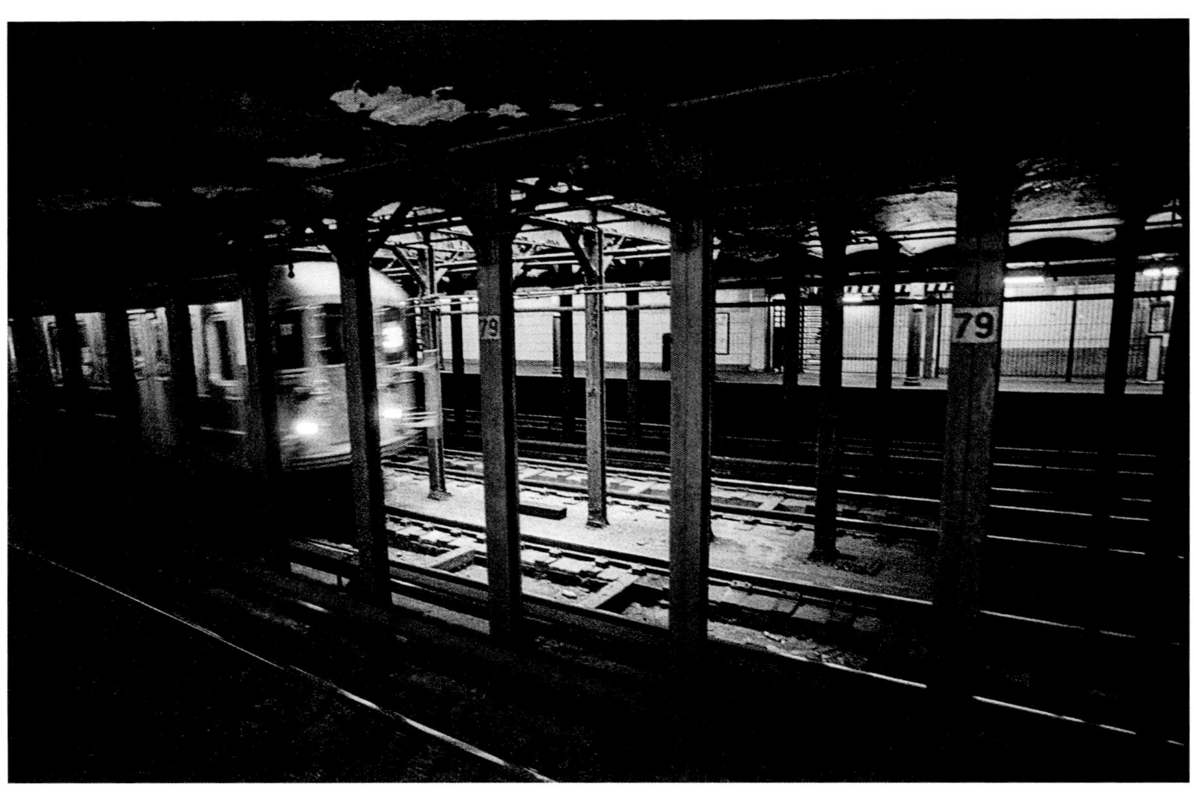
79
79

Reflections on the NYC Subway

–Ed Hotchkiss

For much of my professional life, my humdrum working day, like the typical commuter's, began and ended on the New York City subway. At rush hour, I entered the Lexington Avenue Express at Grand Central and exited at Wall Street. I considered the trip to be Sisyphean labor. I had to negotiate the crowds, the heat, the noise, only to do it again each evening.

When I started this project, the New York City subway was in a state of recovery after two decades of run-down cars, widespread graffiti, and intermittent crime. As I first descended those grimy steps, I knew things had improved, but wasn't sure what I would experience. I kept my head down, avoided making eye contact, and considered myself lucky not to get hassled. However, I found that the system was reasonably safe on all lines, even though taking someone's photo could be perceived as hostile.

As I crisscrossed the city, I realized the subway is the only place where New Yorkers of every status, age, and ethnicity come together in a small, enclosed space. To observe my fellow riders, I was the epitome of anonymity (though I'm sure some thought I was an undercover cop). My uniform was a rumpled black leather jacket, well-worn jeans, and a baseball cap. I would stand or sit with a newspaper in hand, sneak furtive glances, and have my camera positioned on my hip or lap, ready to discreetly snap a shot, often using a cable-release shutter. This approach let me witness my subterranean world without troubling its inhabitants.

In my decade-long odyssey through the New York City subway system, I've traveled every line, to every terminus, many times. I've been surprised by the special worlds I've ended up in. The end of the A line at Far Rockaway in Queens reveals an isolated shore community of windswept streets and weathered bungalows. The elevated train rattles the neighborhood of Brighton Beach in Brooklyn where Cyrillic letters identify shops catering to former residents of the defunct Soviet Republic. Taking the 1 train to Van Cortlandt Park in the Bronx and watching the camaraderie of cricket players reminds me of the softball games of my Denver childhood.

As I rode, I began to see moments, gestures, expressions of interactions. I began to interpret stories from seemingly insignificant details—laugh lines around a person's mouth, a defiant stance, or the spring in someone's step. Whether it's the day-to-day grind of commuting, the joy of riding the train with a new love, or the chore of simply living your life and getting where you need to go, the subway is a large part of life for most New Yorkers.

Lights define and shape what I see underground. A seconds-long glimpse through an illuminated train window is just enough for me to wonder about a passenger's destination in the subterranean darkness. I quickly capture it on film, hoping that I will see even more in the finished print. The lights of an approaching train are infinitely promising. Those of a departing one make me feel left behind and lonely. I sometimes imagine that the red lights, the train and the people in it simply disappear after they leave the station.

You can't hear the transit sounds in my images, but they're there, just the same. If you're waiting on a platform and you're late for an appointment, you are listening for that coming train two stations away. It's a faraway rumble, a distant promise. Is it the "clacketaclacketaclack" of the local or the "throom" of an express train that will pass you by? The chug of the train traveling through the tunnel ends in the screech of brakes. Then there's the breathy sound of the doors opening and the hiccupping sound as they try to close again and again. Then the puff-puff escape of air as the train gets started on its weary way to the next fluorescent oasis.

Now each examination of my contact sheets is a trip down memory lane. Two teens embrace and stare intently into each other's eyes, oblivious to everyone around them, or perhaps not. A protective mother takes her sleeping kids somewhere: home? the doctor? the in-laws'? A man on his way home from work, clearly in the sunset of his life, has probably been riding the subways for decades. Hundreds of rolls and thousands of images later, clearer patterns emerge. Some of the images and impressions from that journey have found their way into this book while others are fixed in my memory.

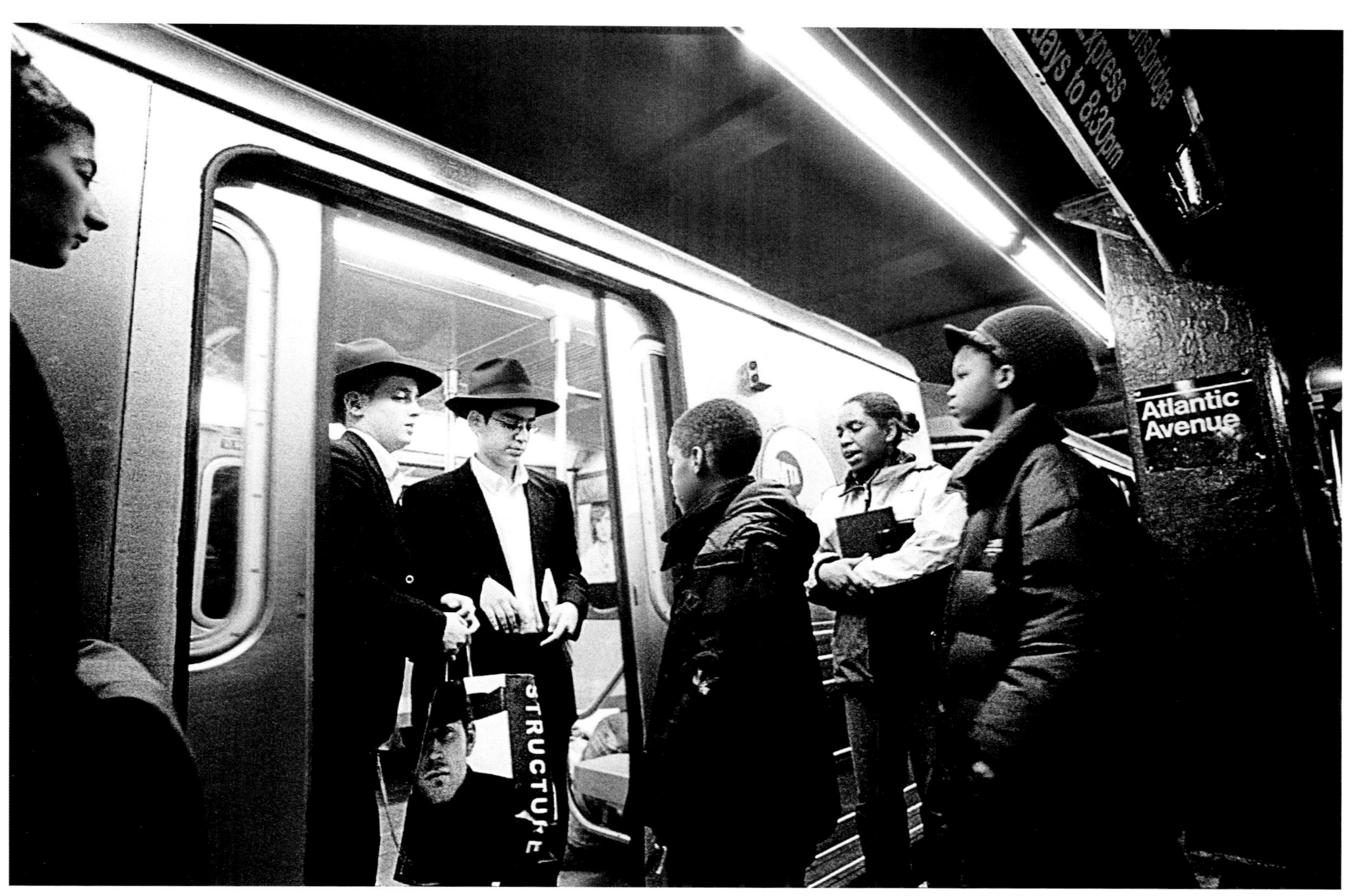
Atlantic
Avenue
STRUCTURE

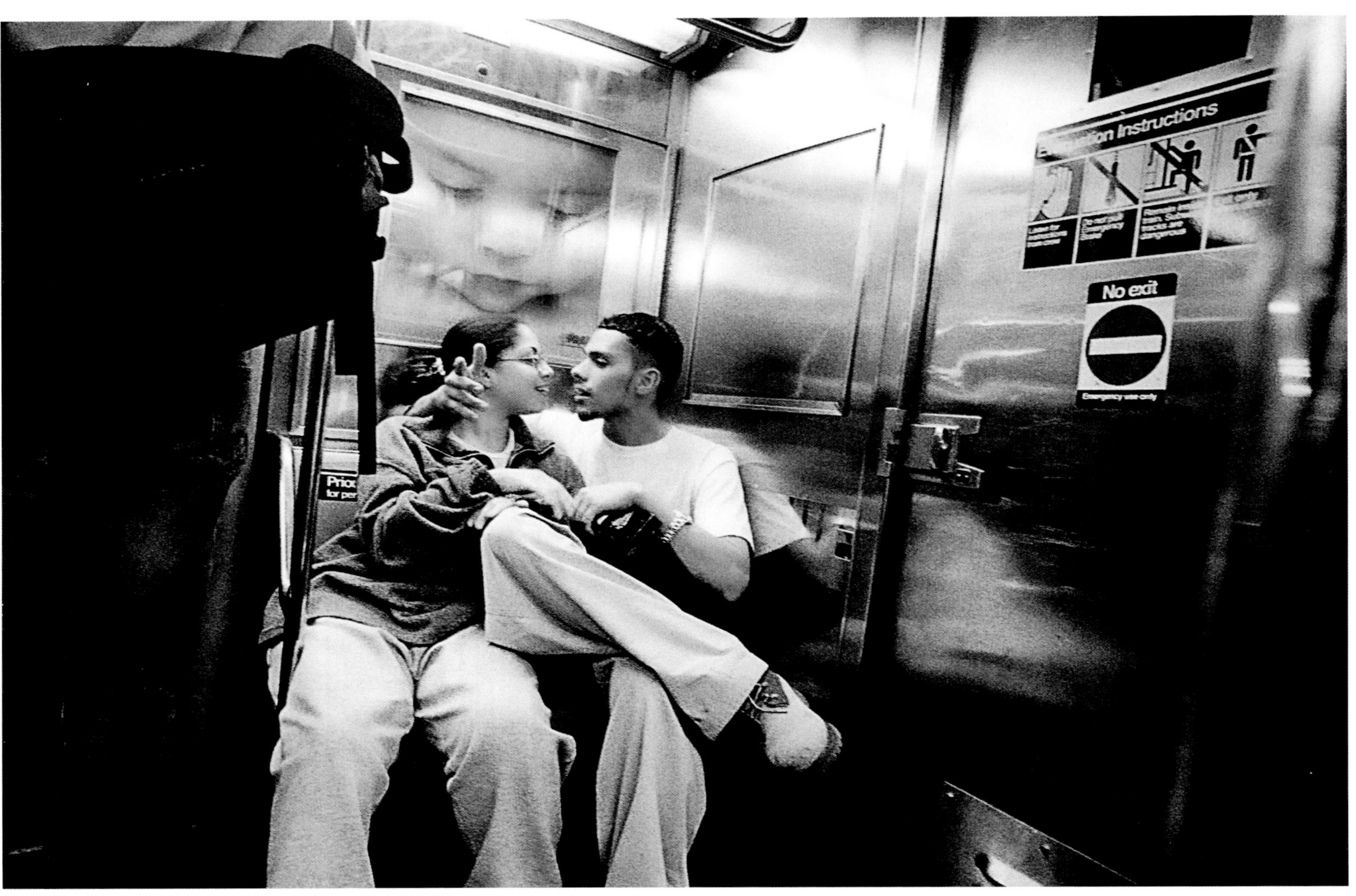
Instructions
No exit
Emergency use only
Priority
for per

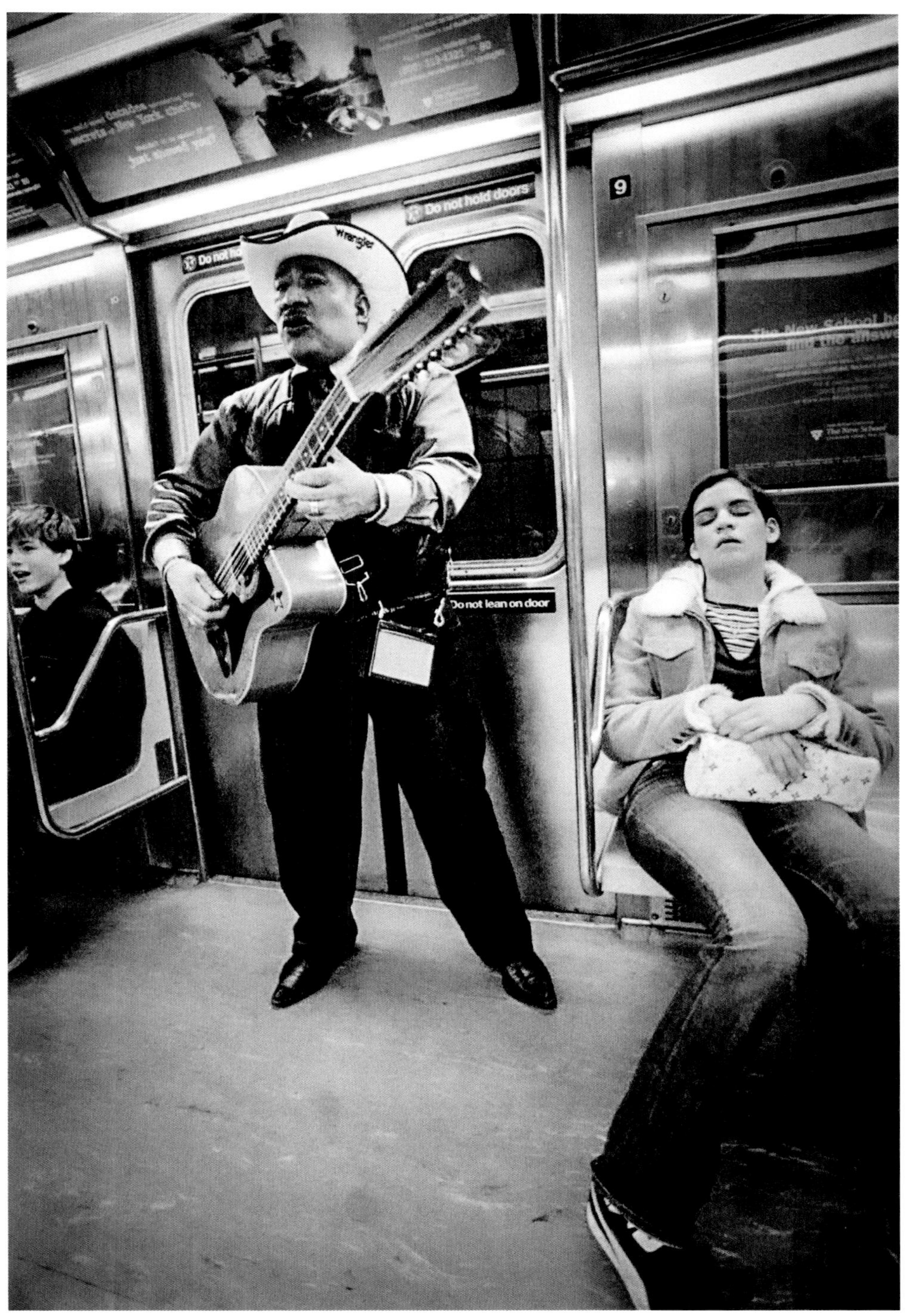
Do not hold doors
Do not lean on door
9

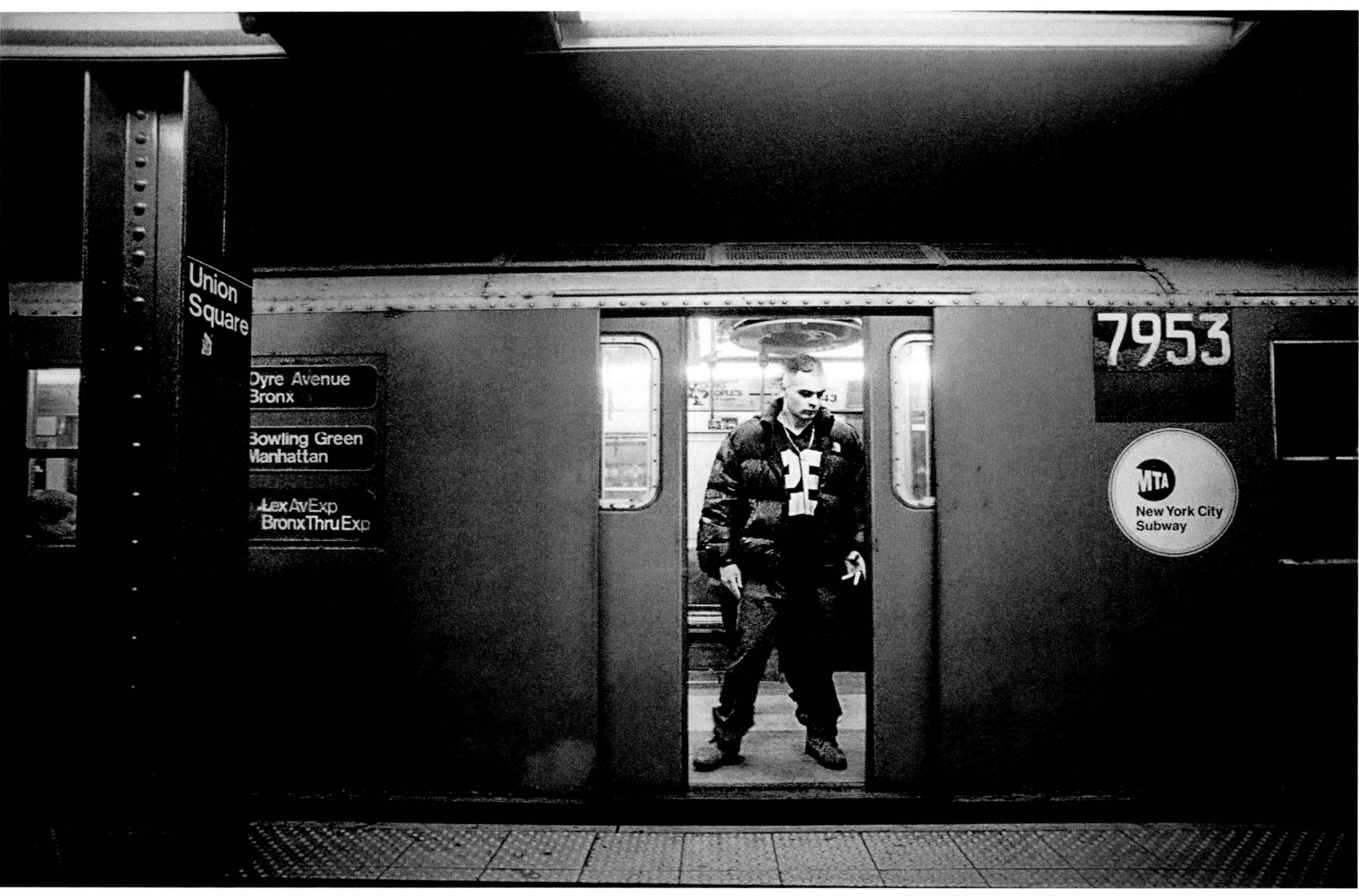

Union
Square
Dyre Avenue
Bronx
Bowling Green
Manhattan
Lex Av Exp
Bronx Thru Exp
7953
MTA
New York City
Subway

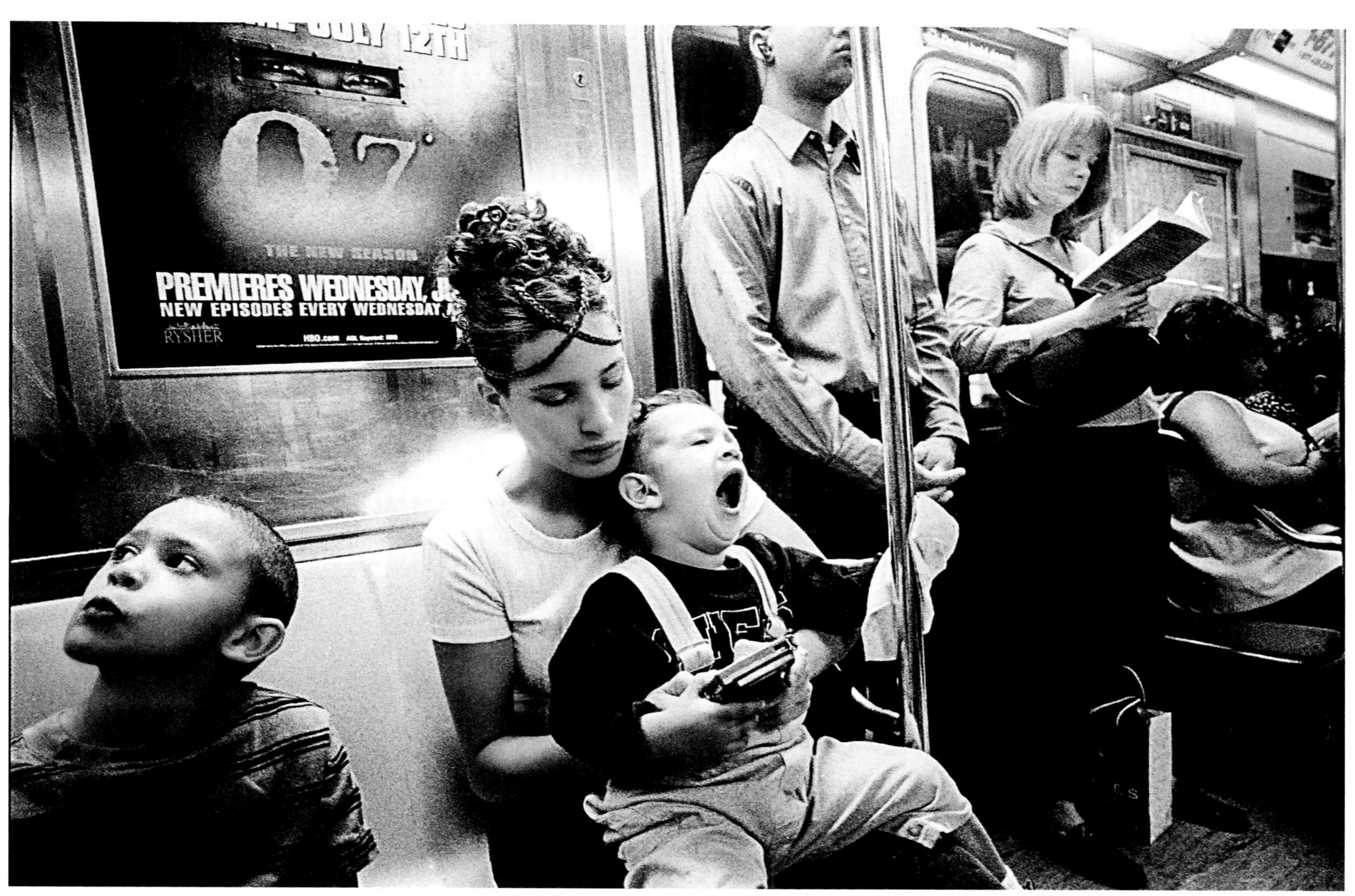
JULY 12TH
OZ
THE NEW SEASON
PREMIERES WEDNESDAY, J
NEW EPISODES EVERY WEDNESDAY,
RYSHER
HBO.com

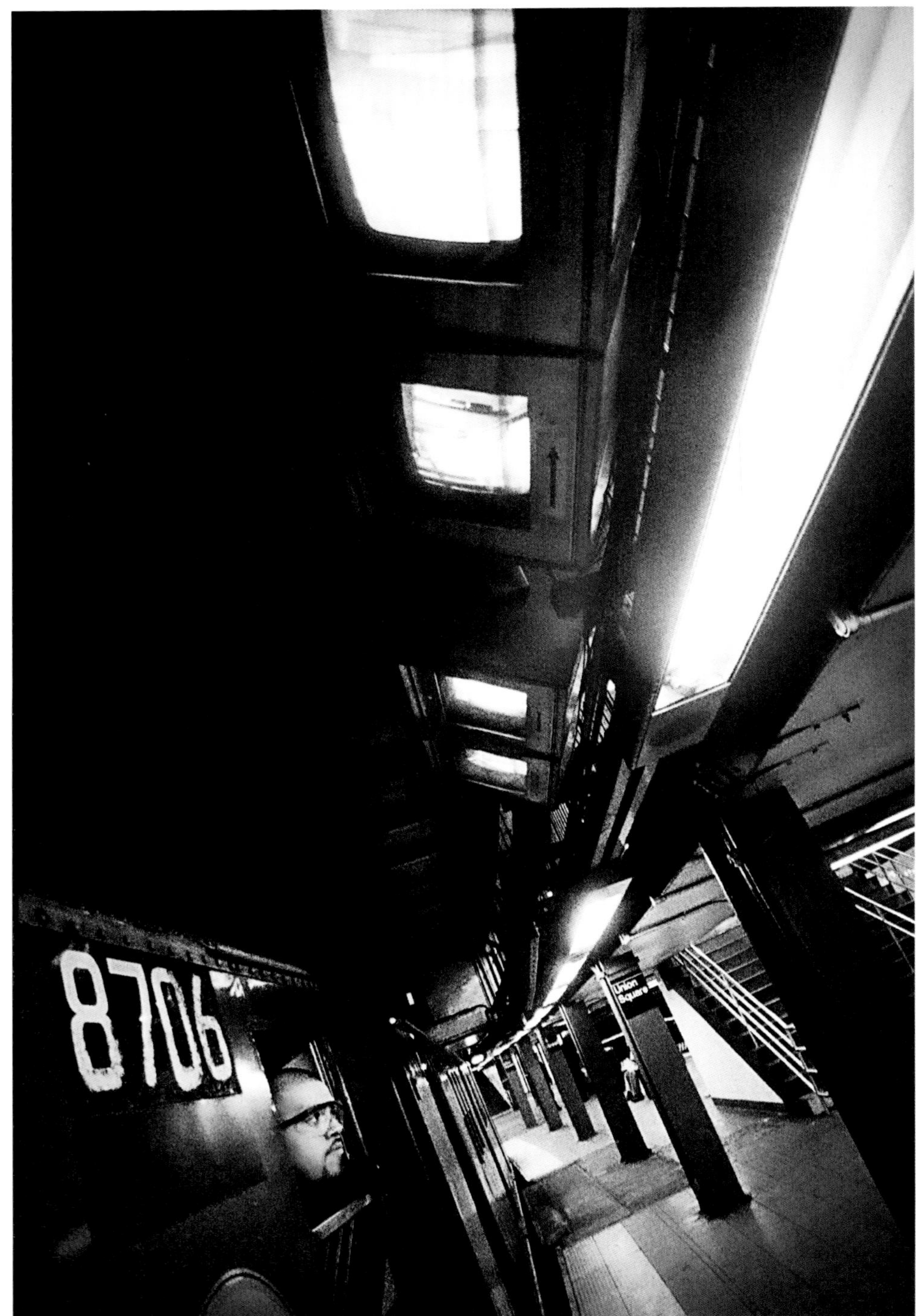
8706
Union
Square

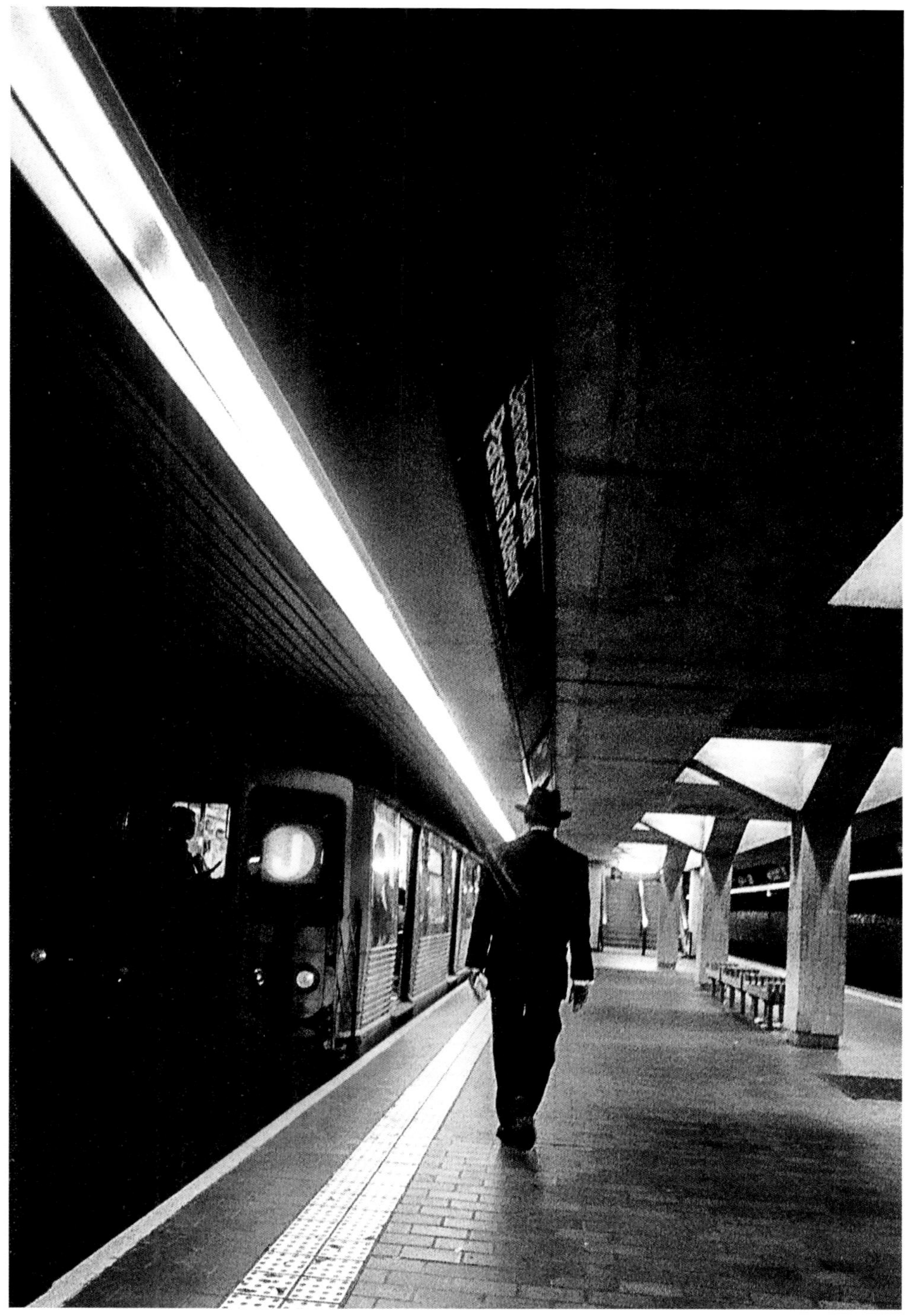

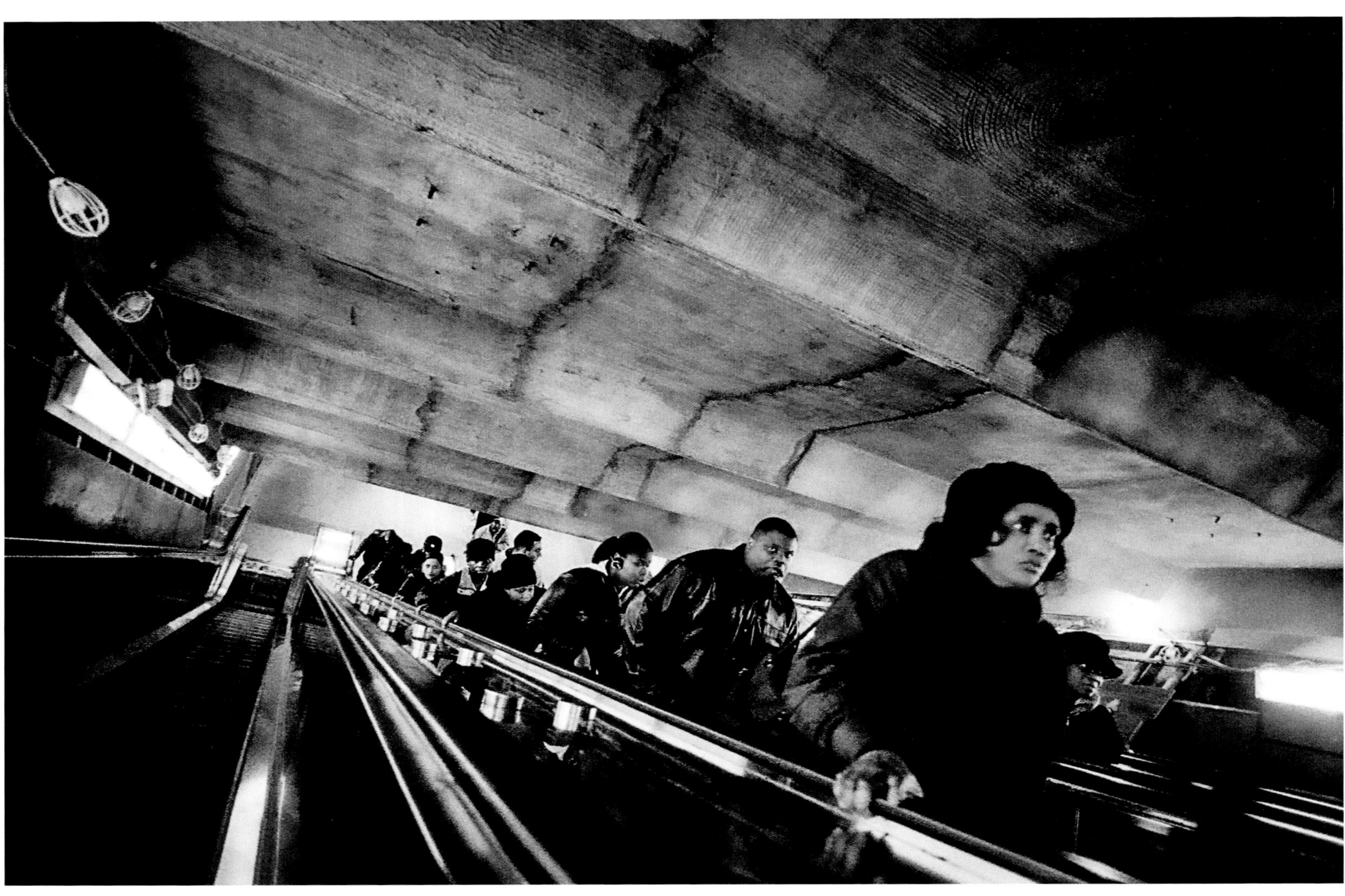

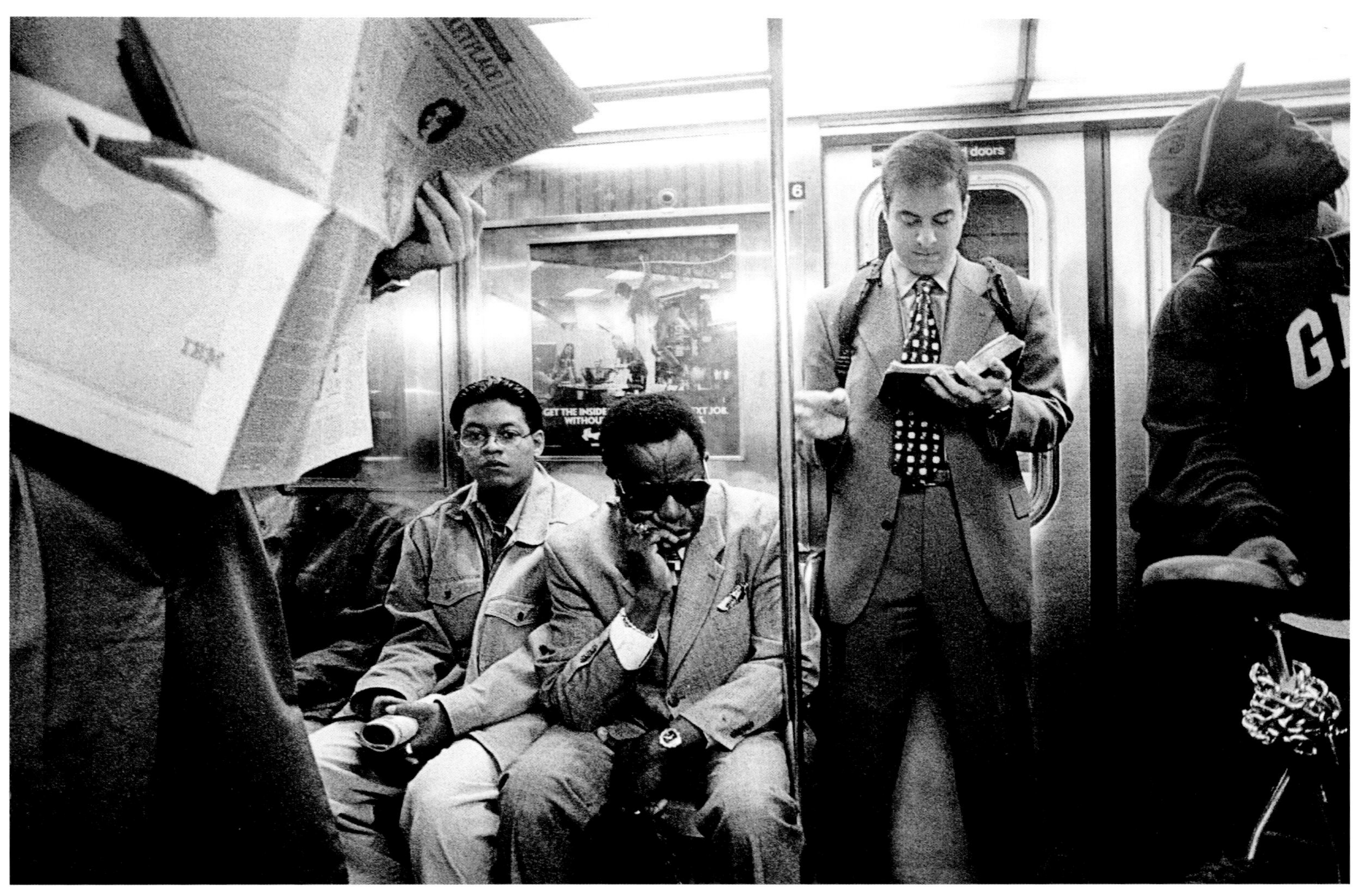

doors
6
GET THE INSIDE
WITHOUT
IBM
G

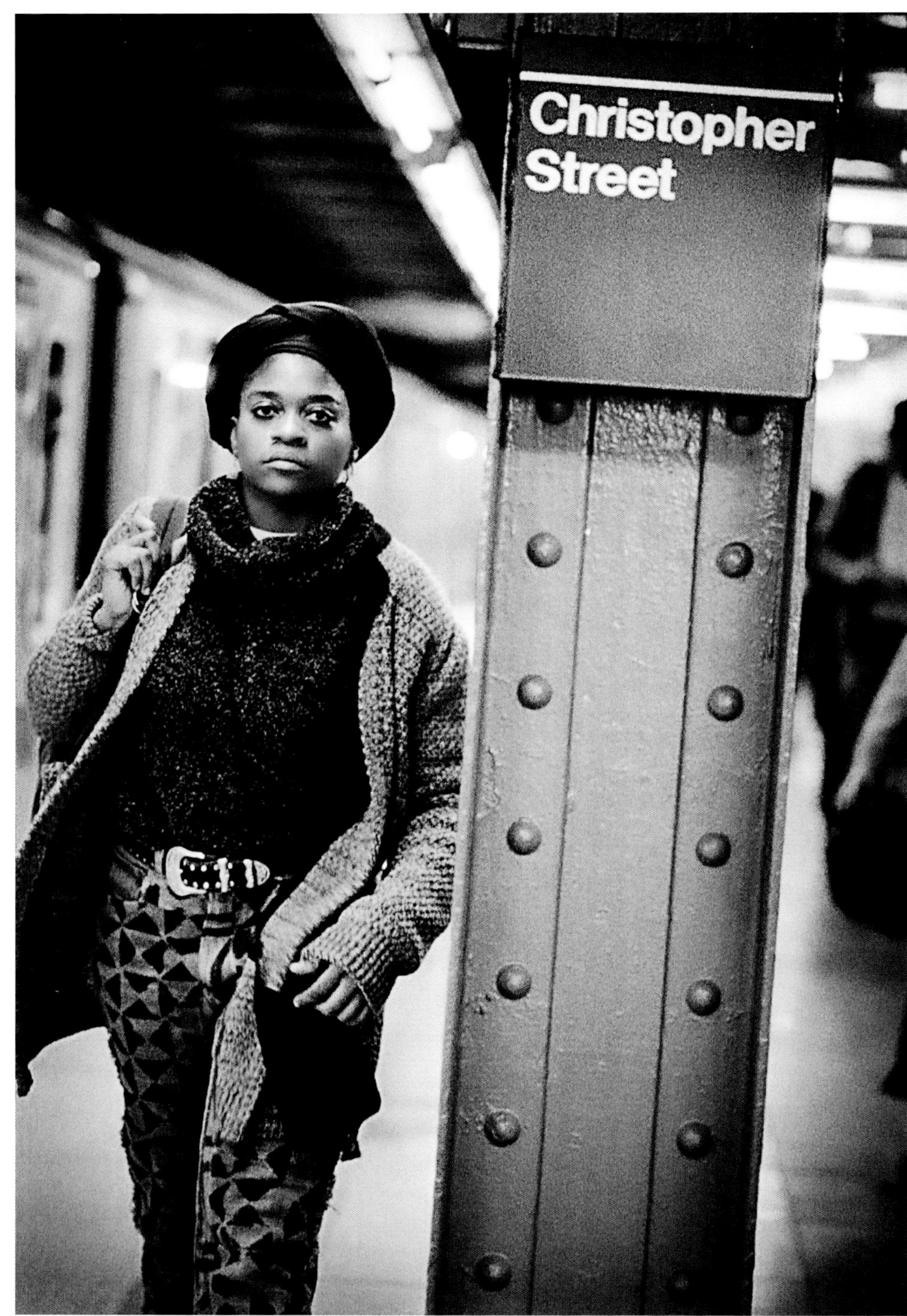

Christopher
Street

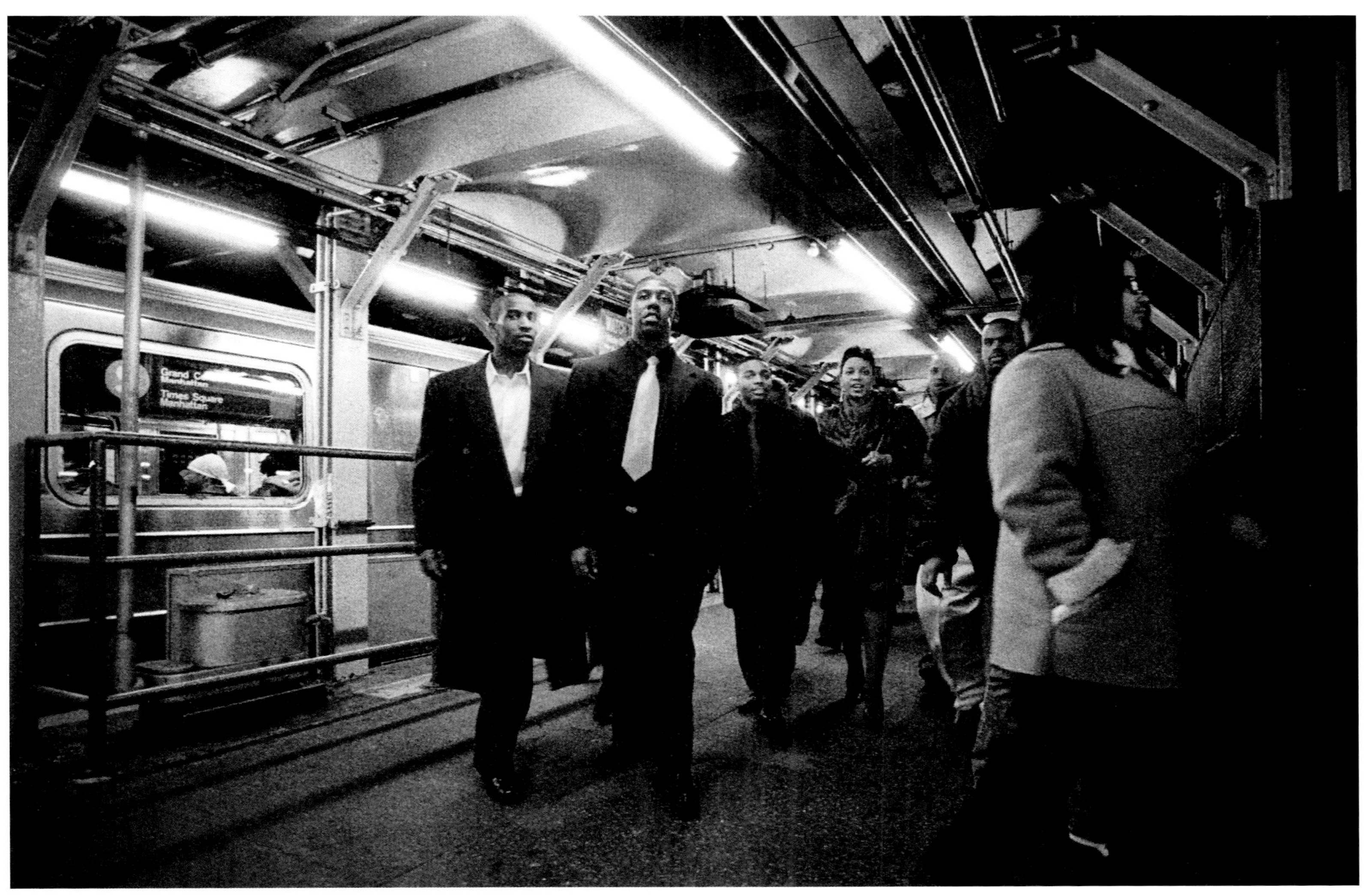

Grand C
Times Square
Manhattan

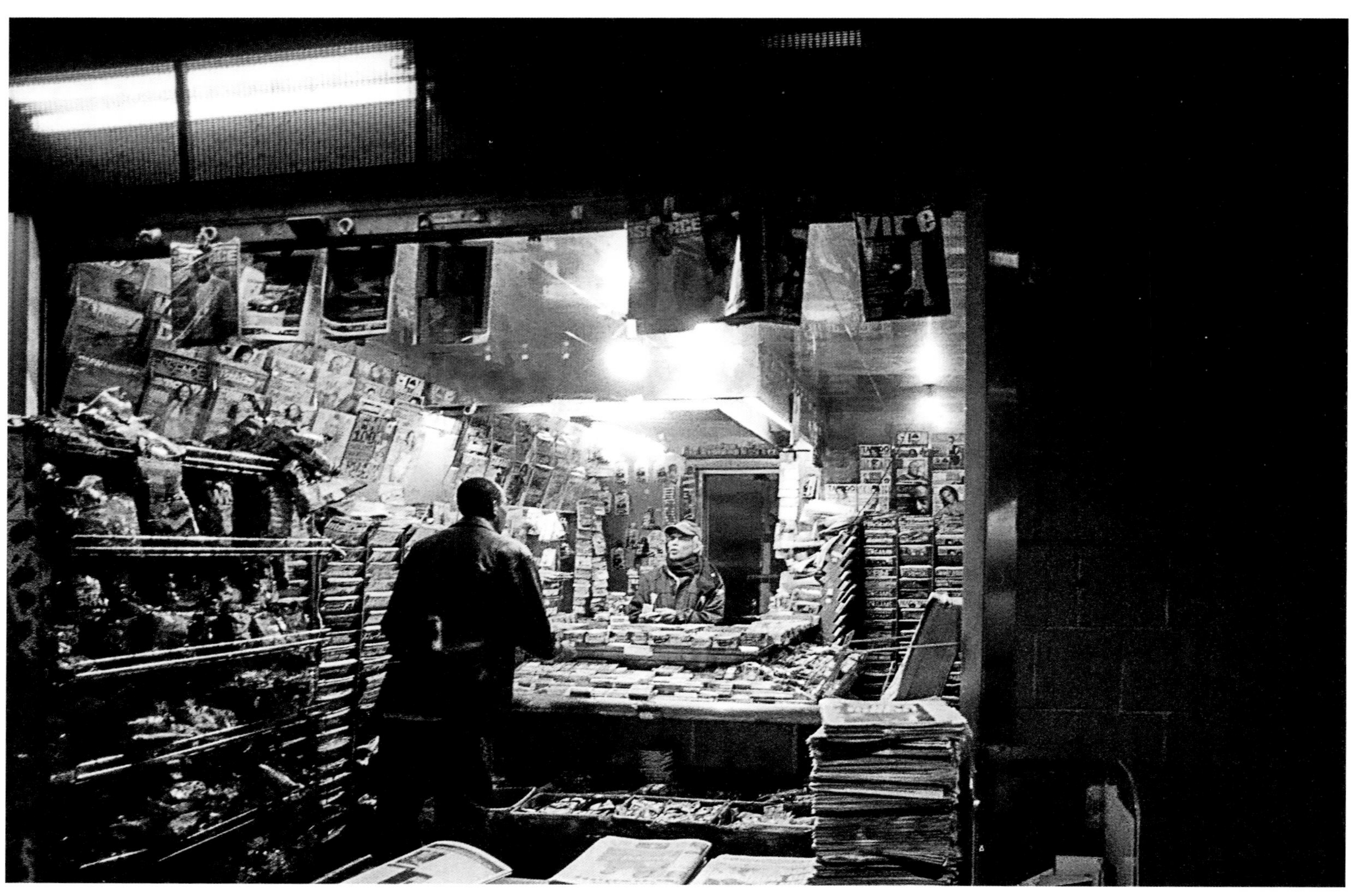

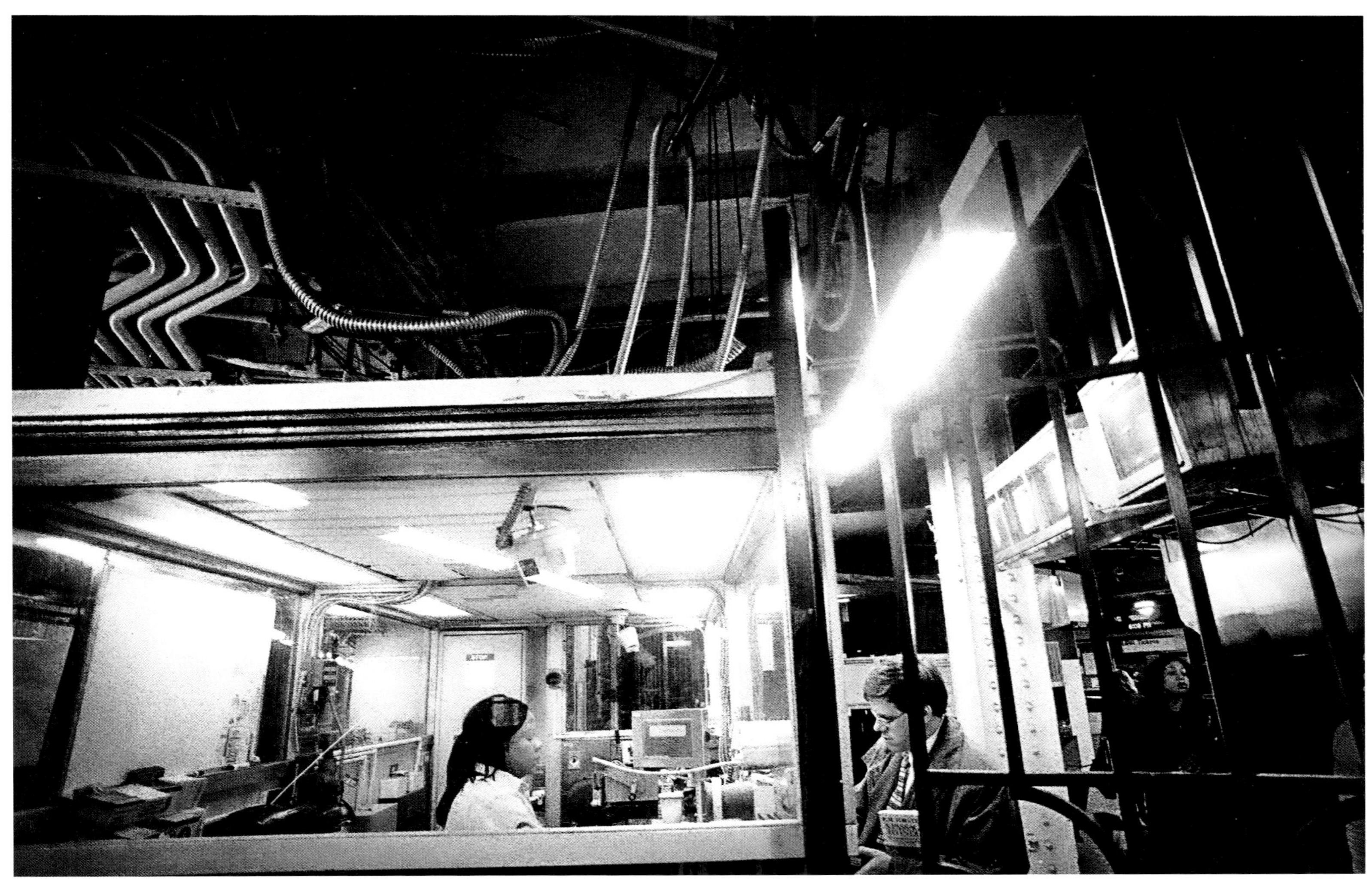

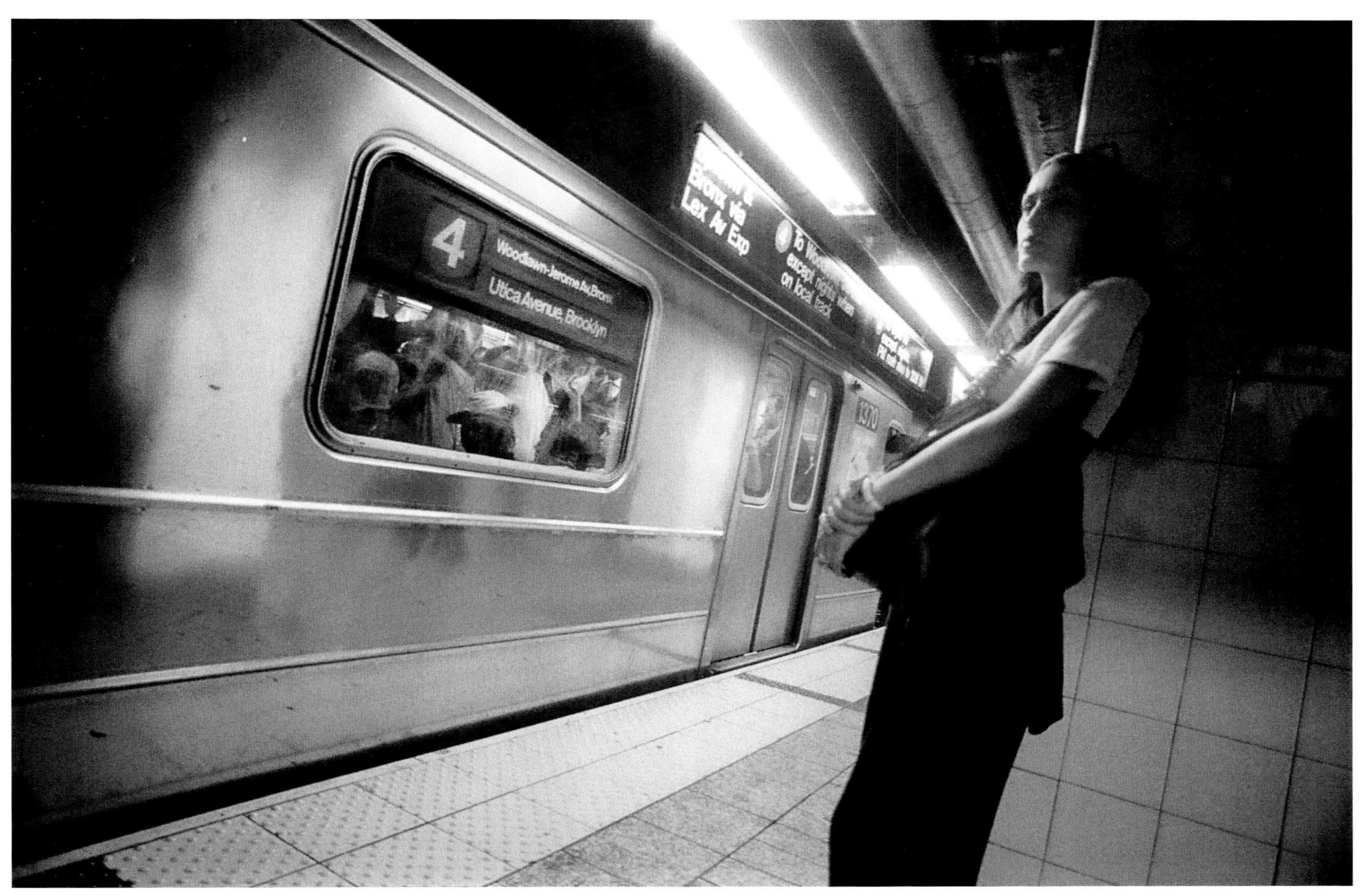

4
Woodlawn-Jerome Av.Bronx
Utica Avenue, Brooklyn
Bronx via
Lex Av Exp
except nights when
on local track

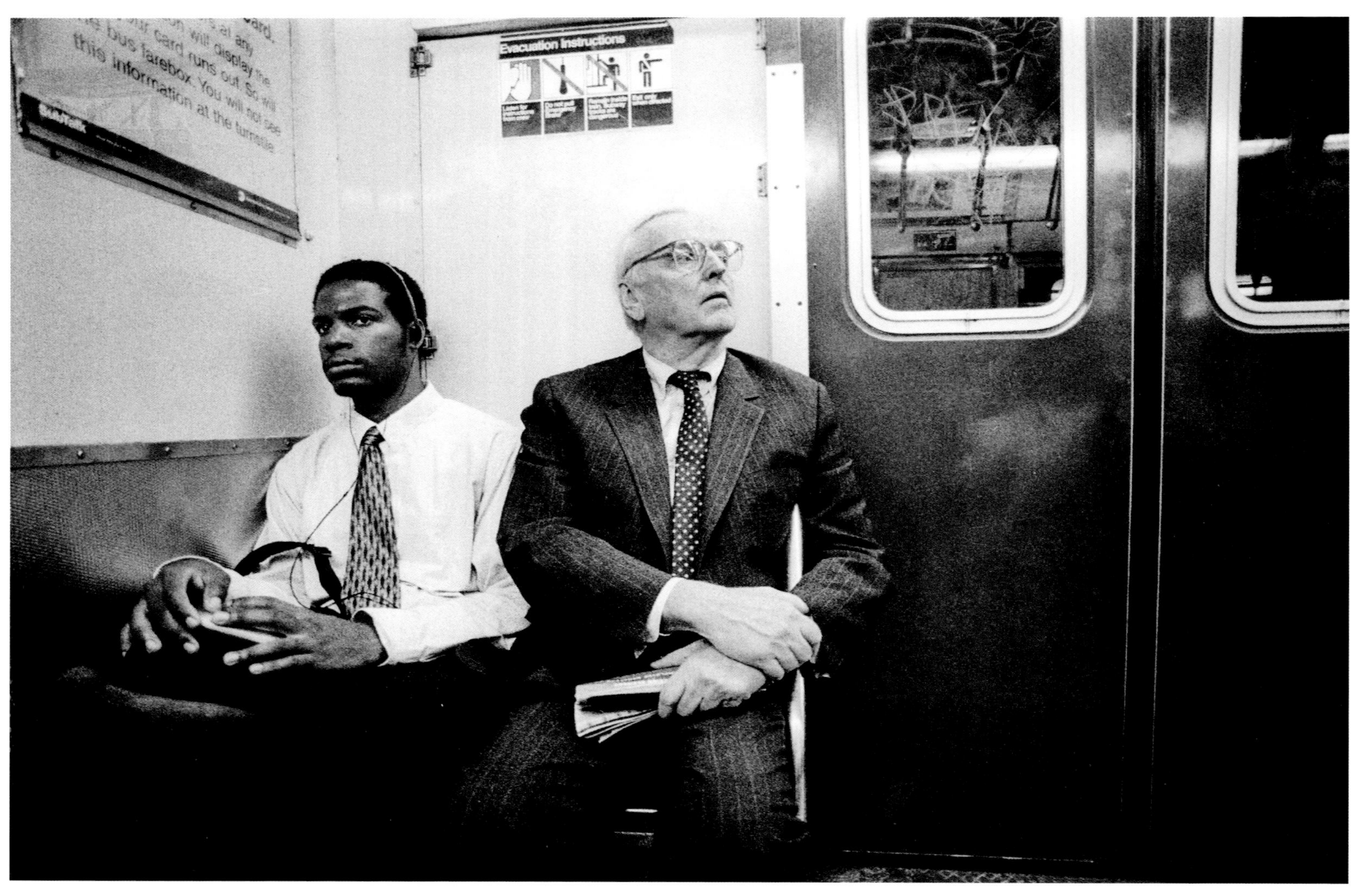

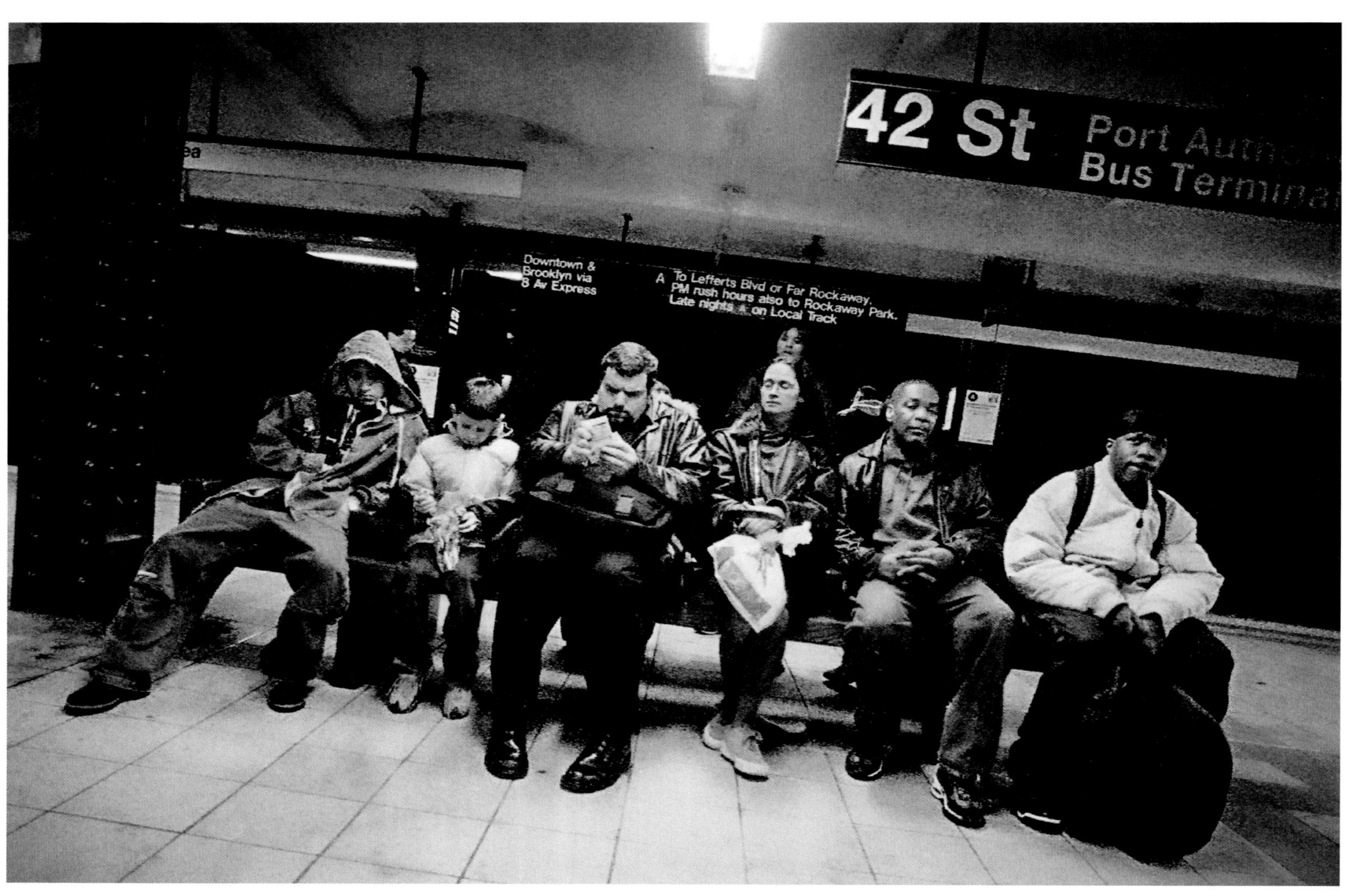
42 St
Port Autho...
Bus Termina...
Downtown &
Brooklyn via
8 Av Express
A To Lefferts Blvd or Far Rockaway.
PM rush hours also to Rockaway Park.
Late nights ★ on Local Track

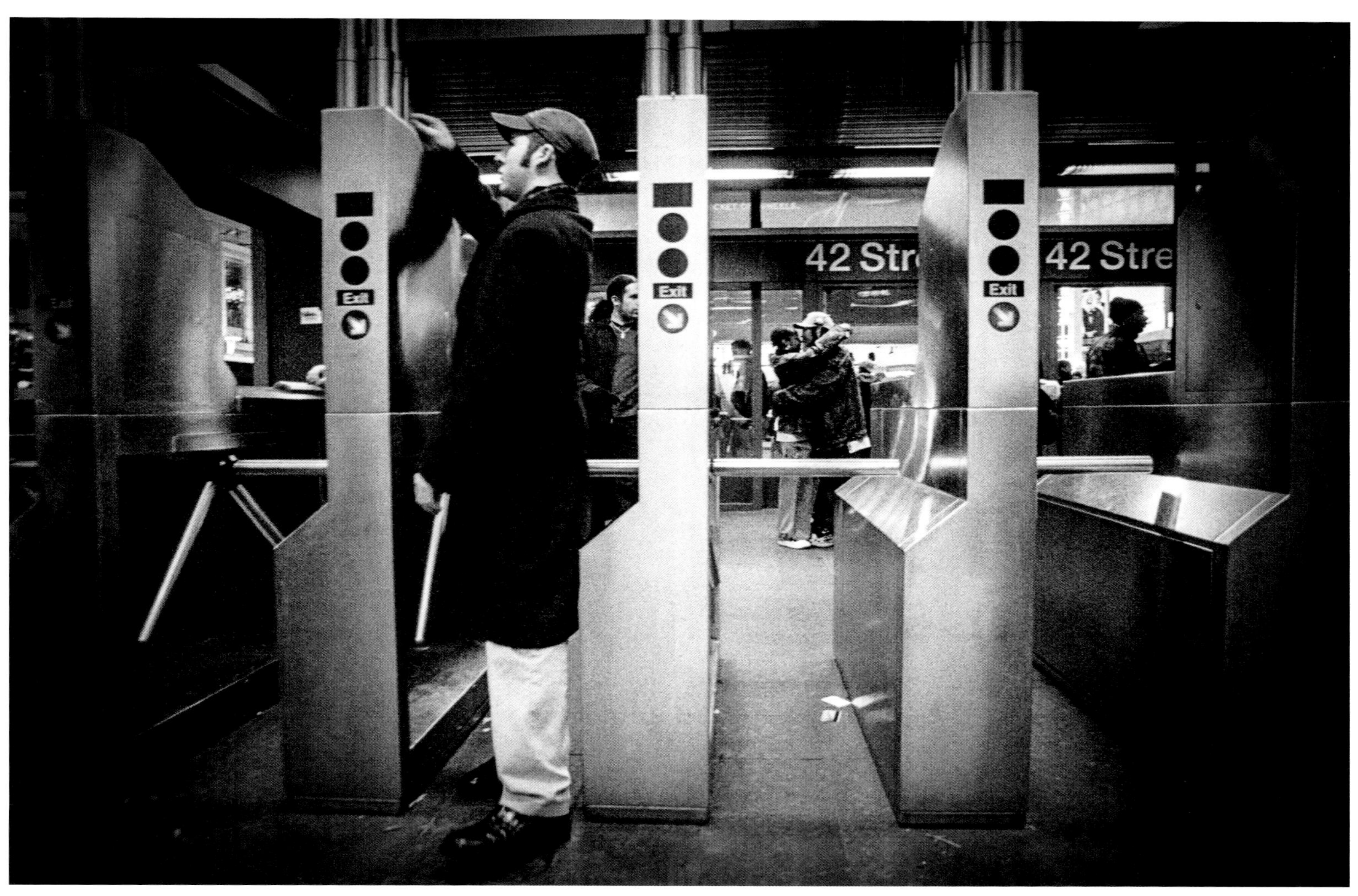
Exit
42 Str
Exit
42 Stre
Exit

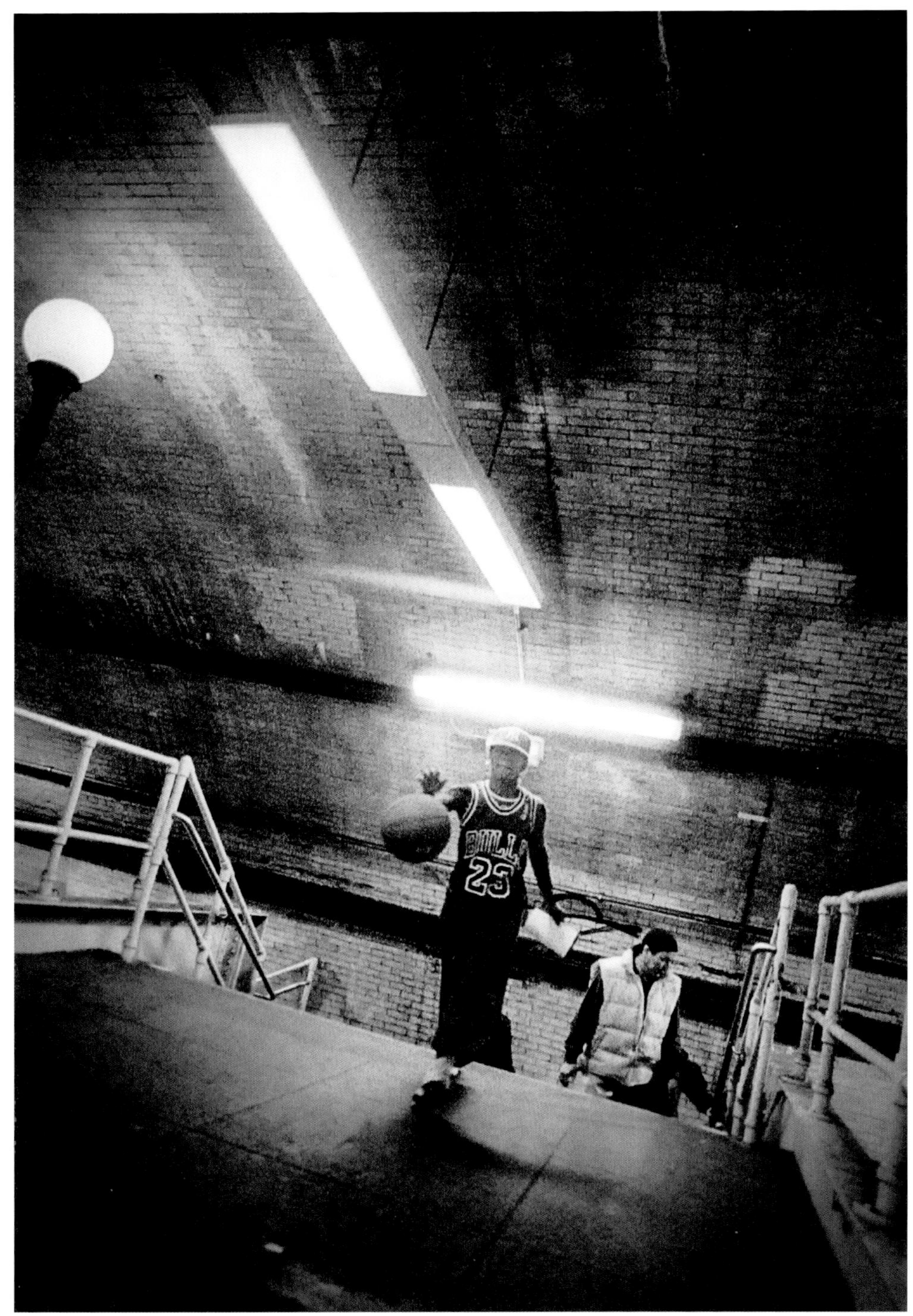

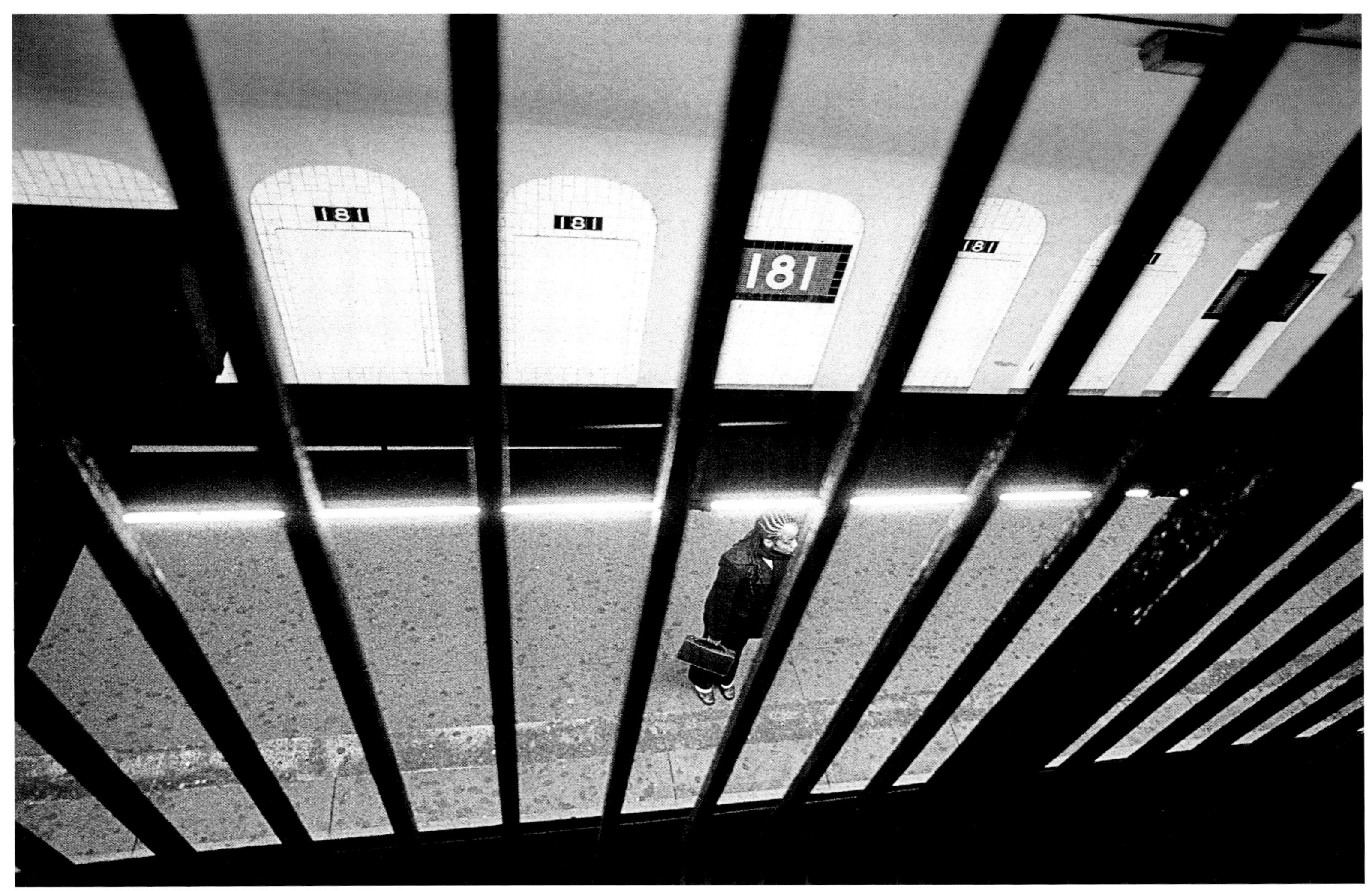
181
181
181
181

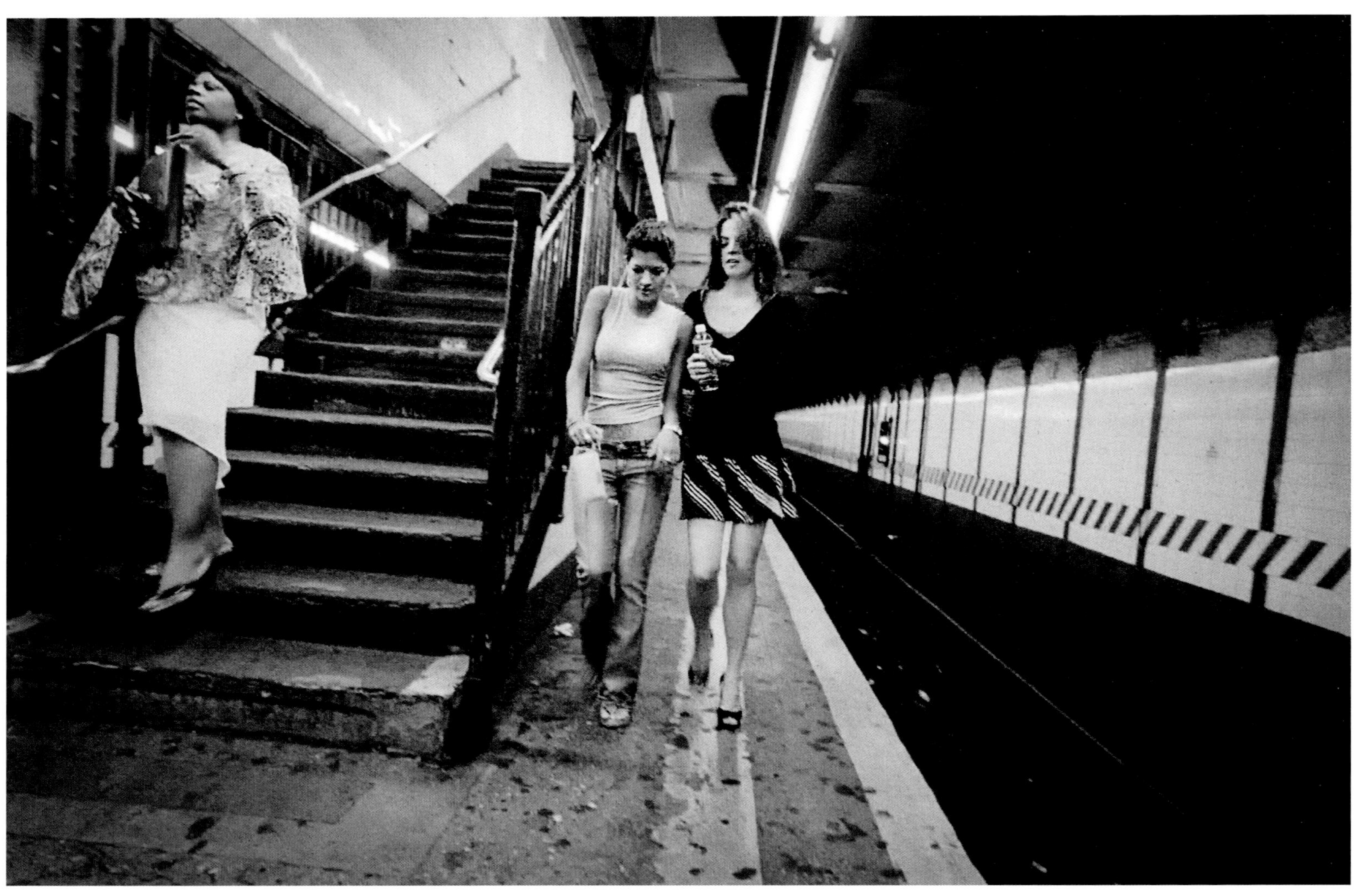

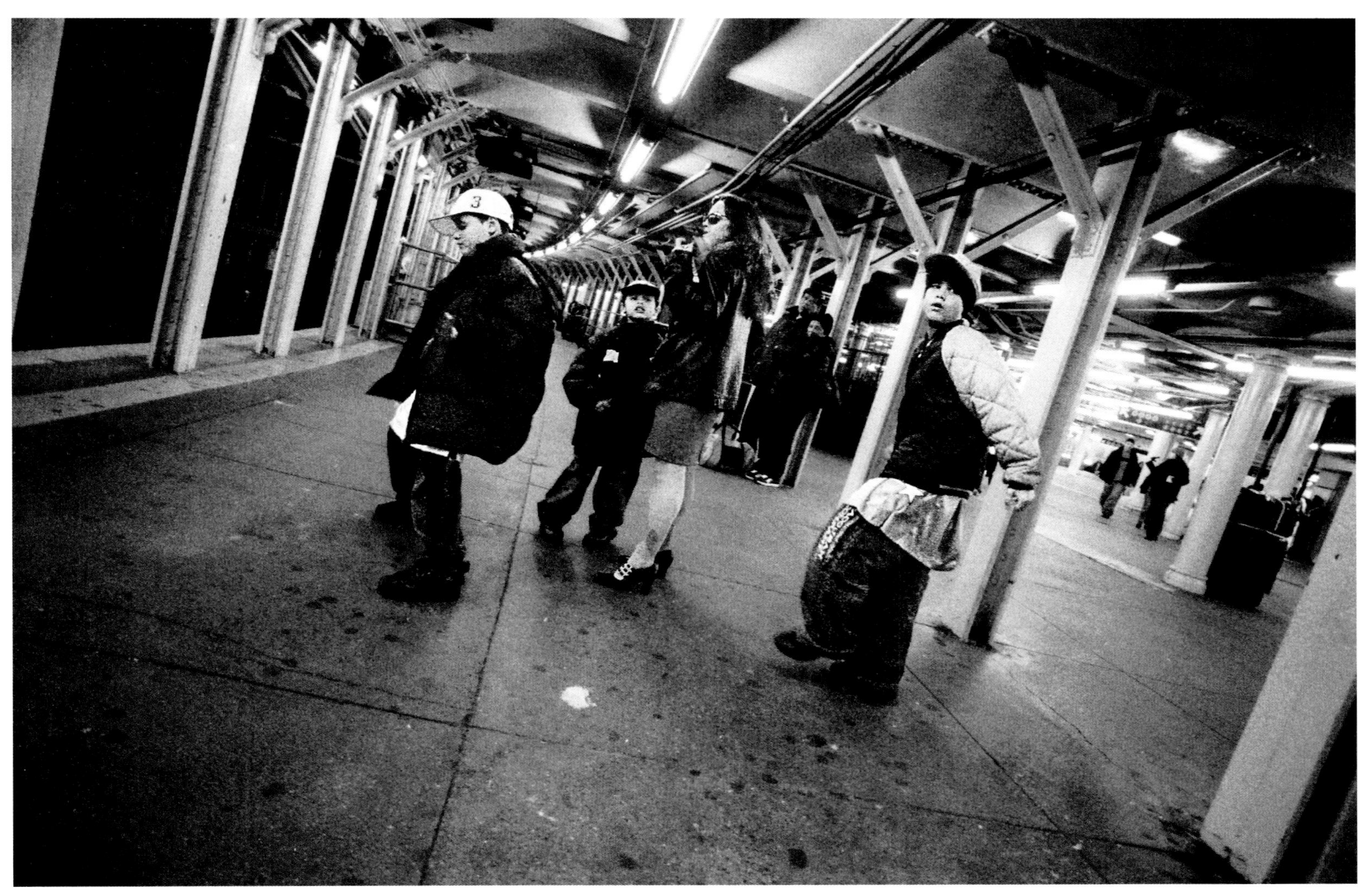

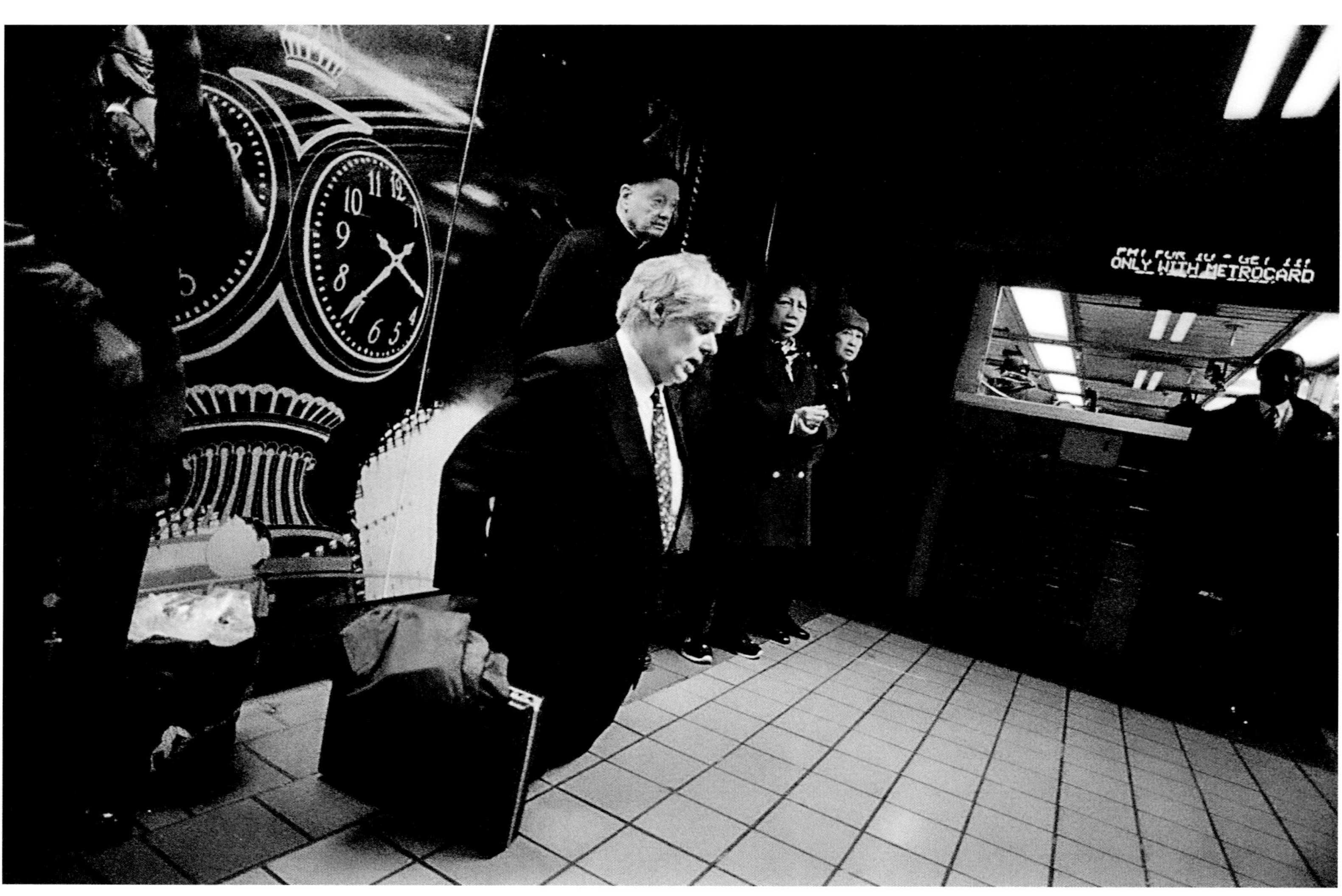

ONLY WITH METROCARD

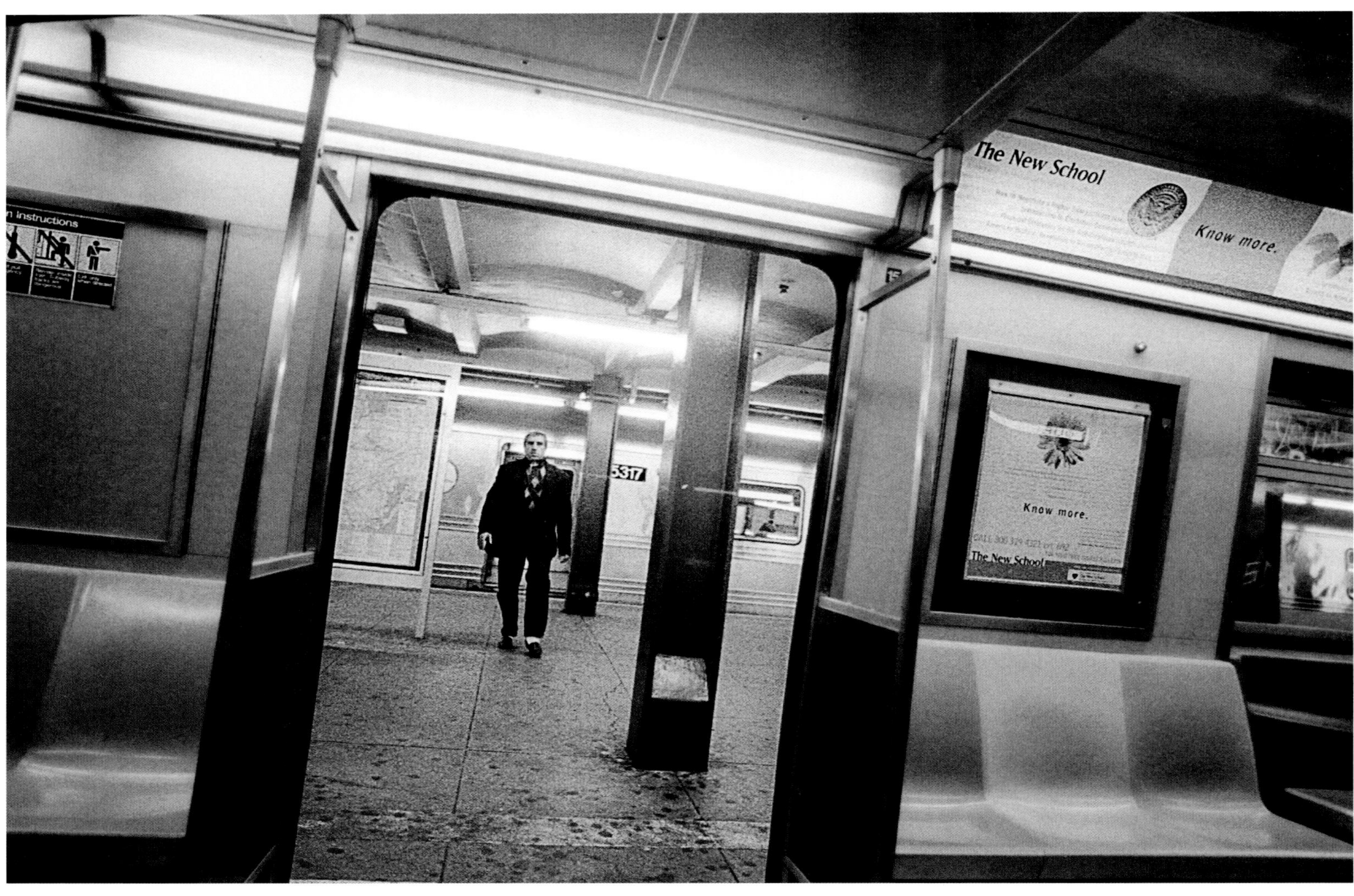
The New School
Know more.
Know more.
The New School

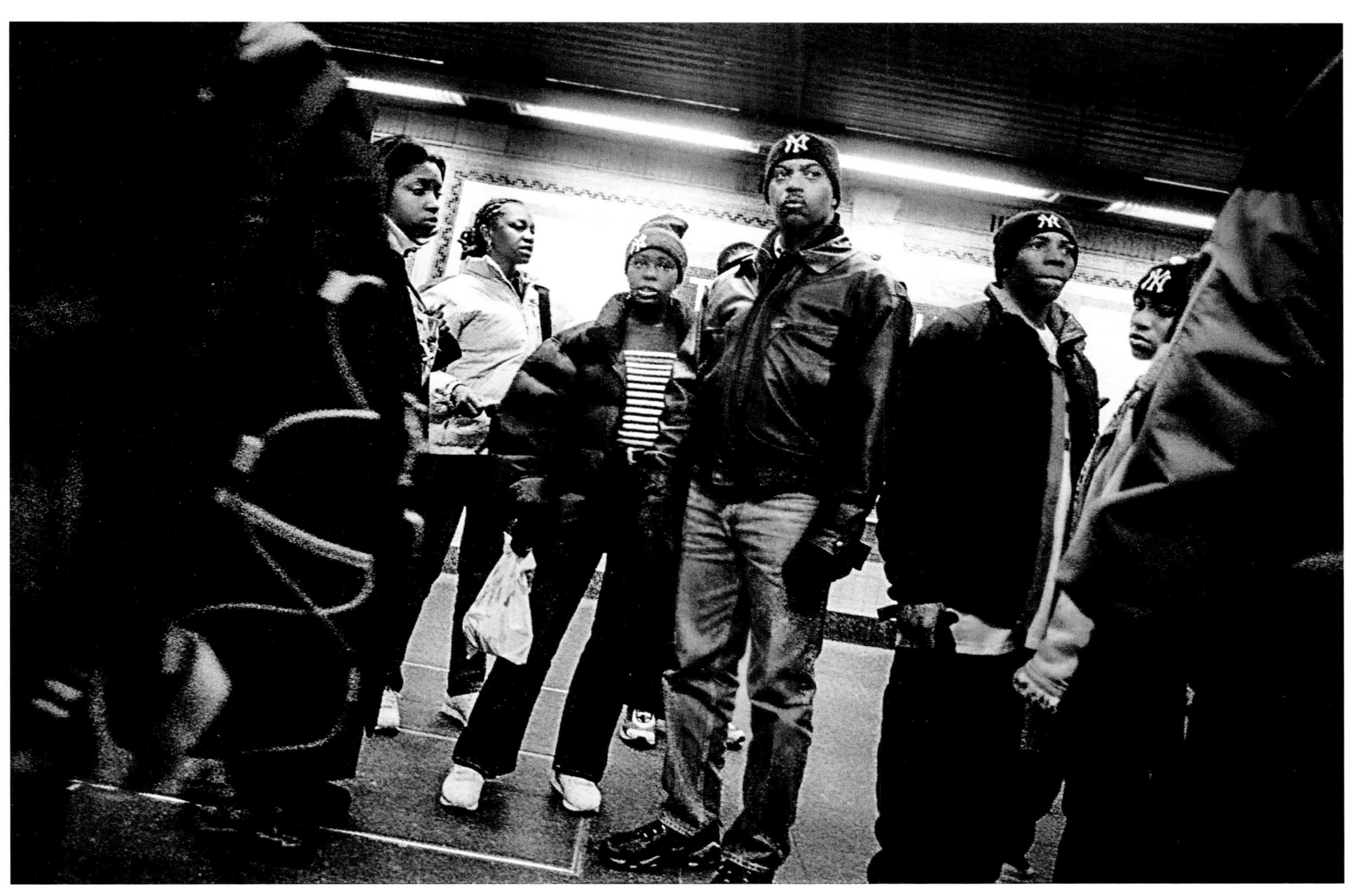

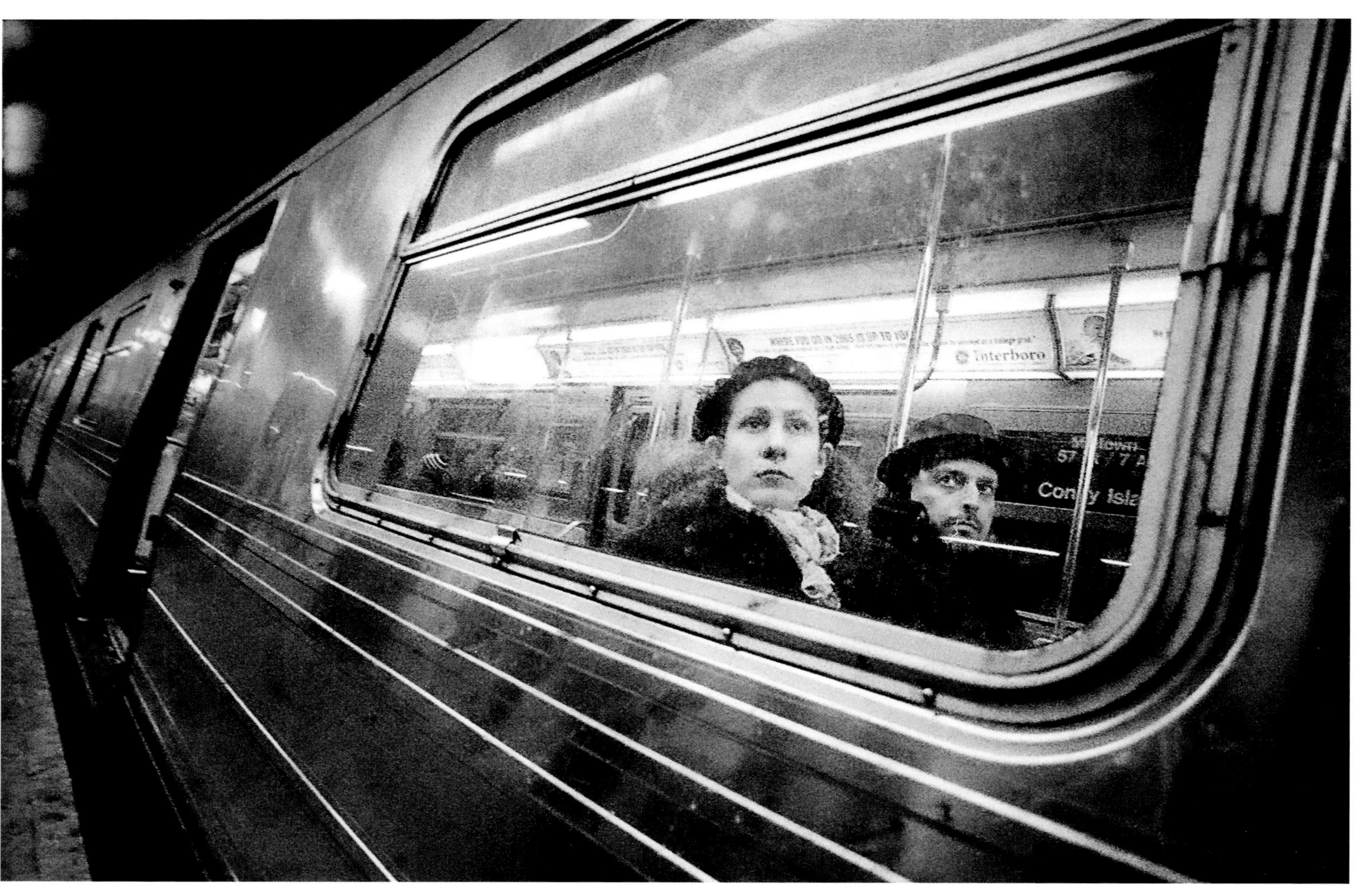
Interboro
Conny Isla

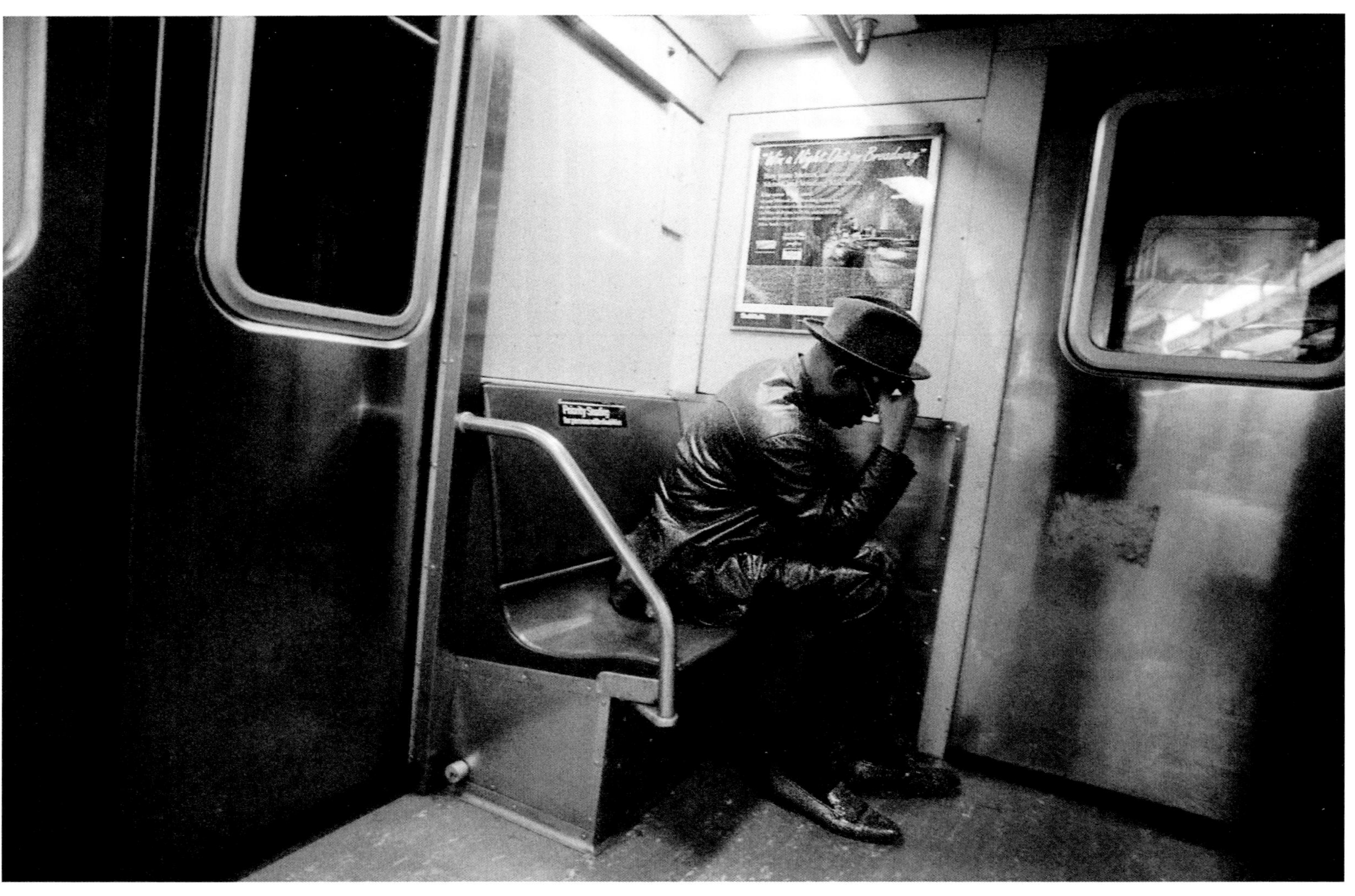

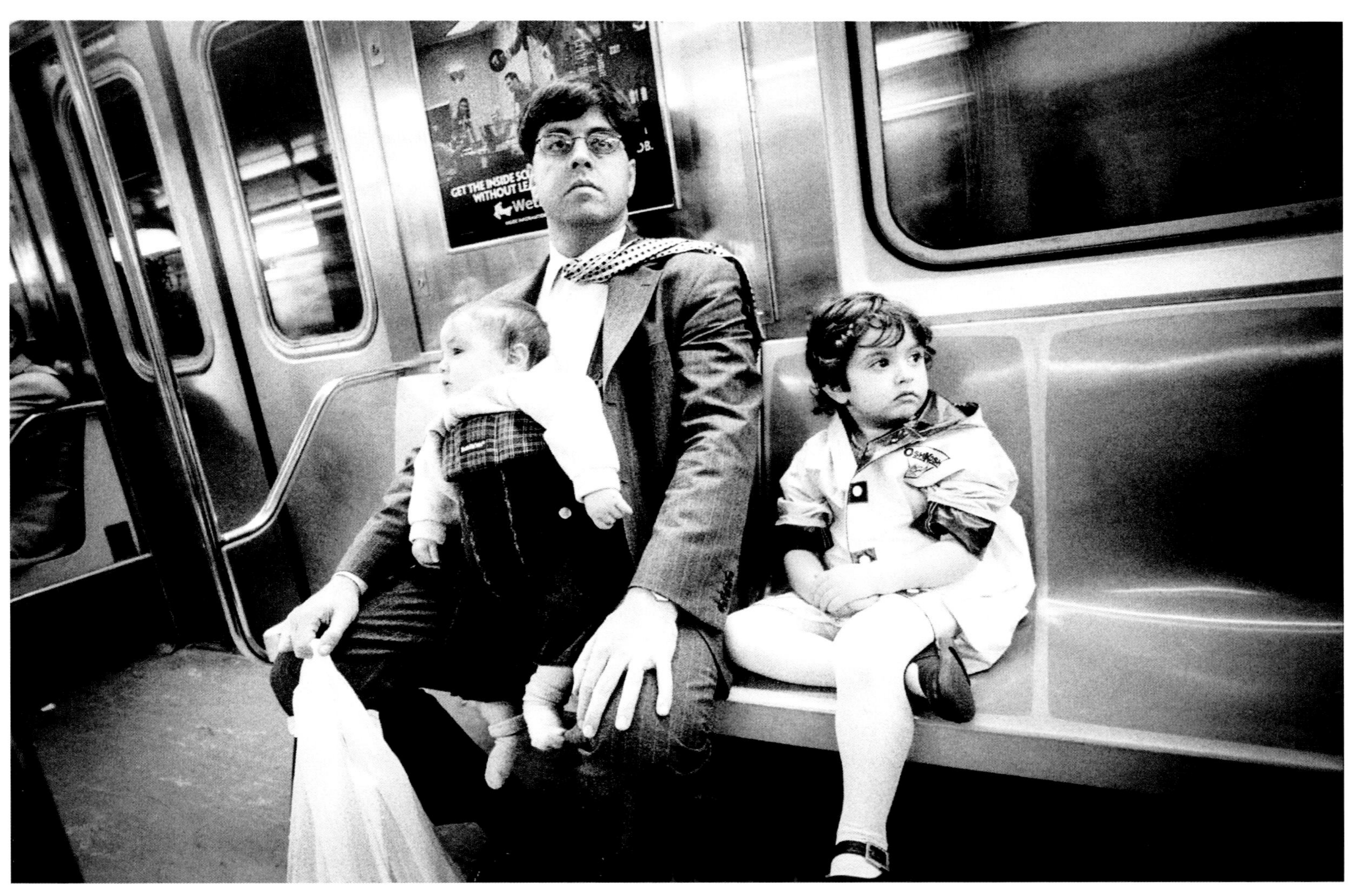

GET THE INSIDE SCO
WITHOUT LE

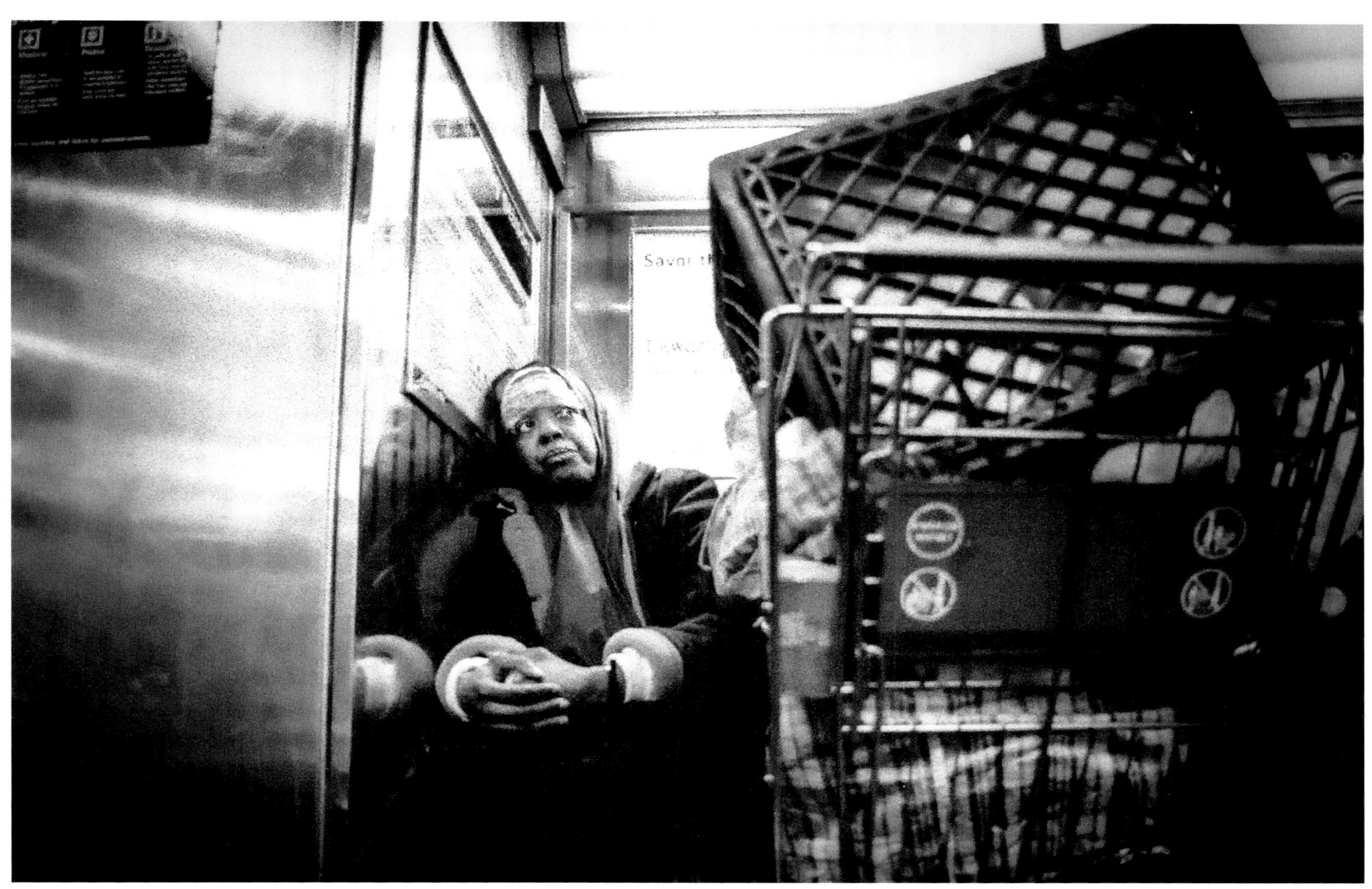

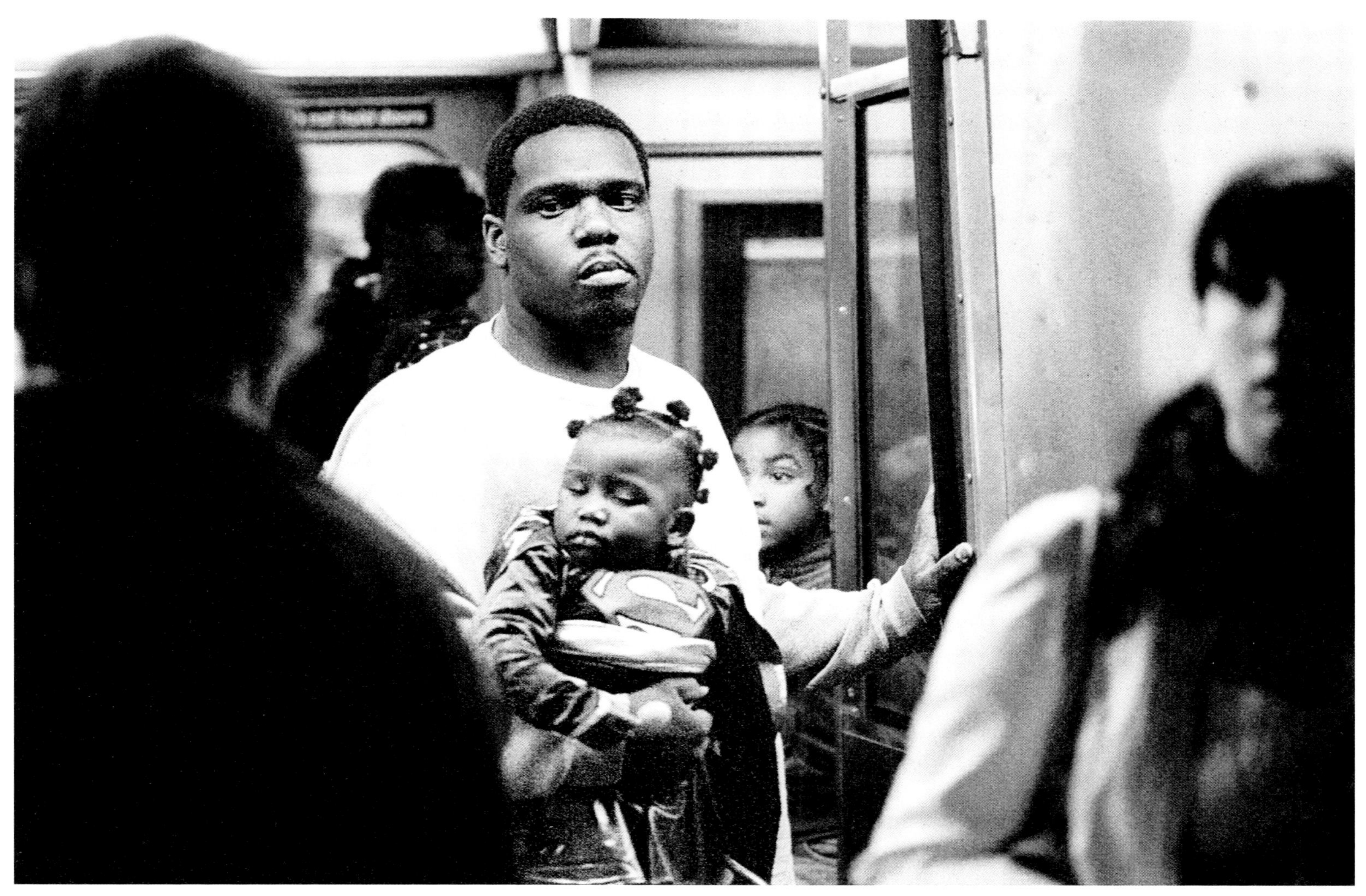

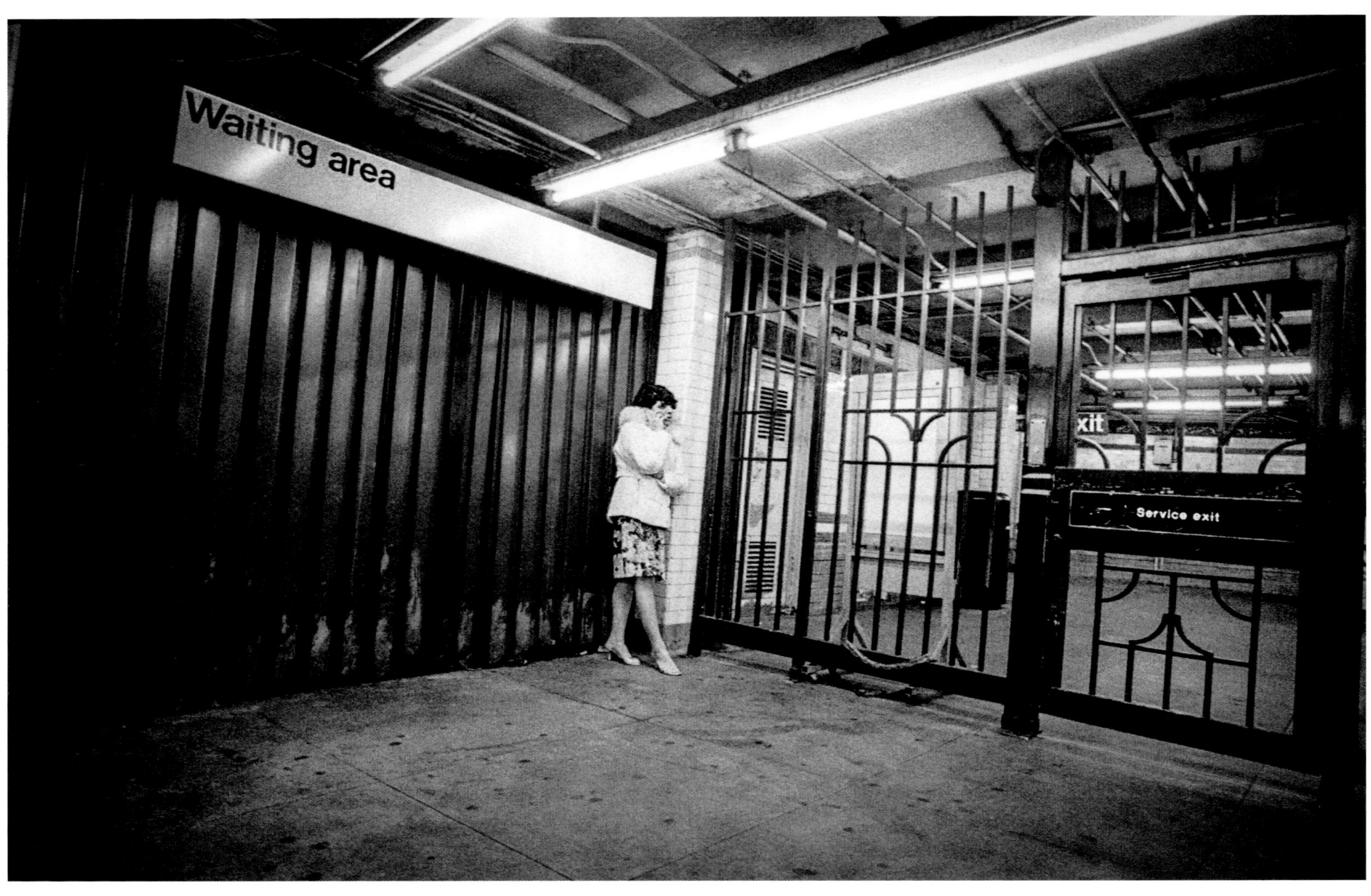
Waiting area
Service exit
xit

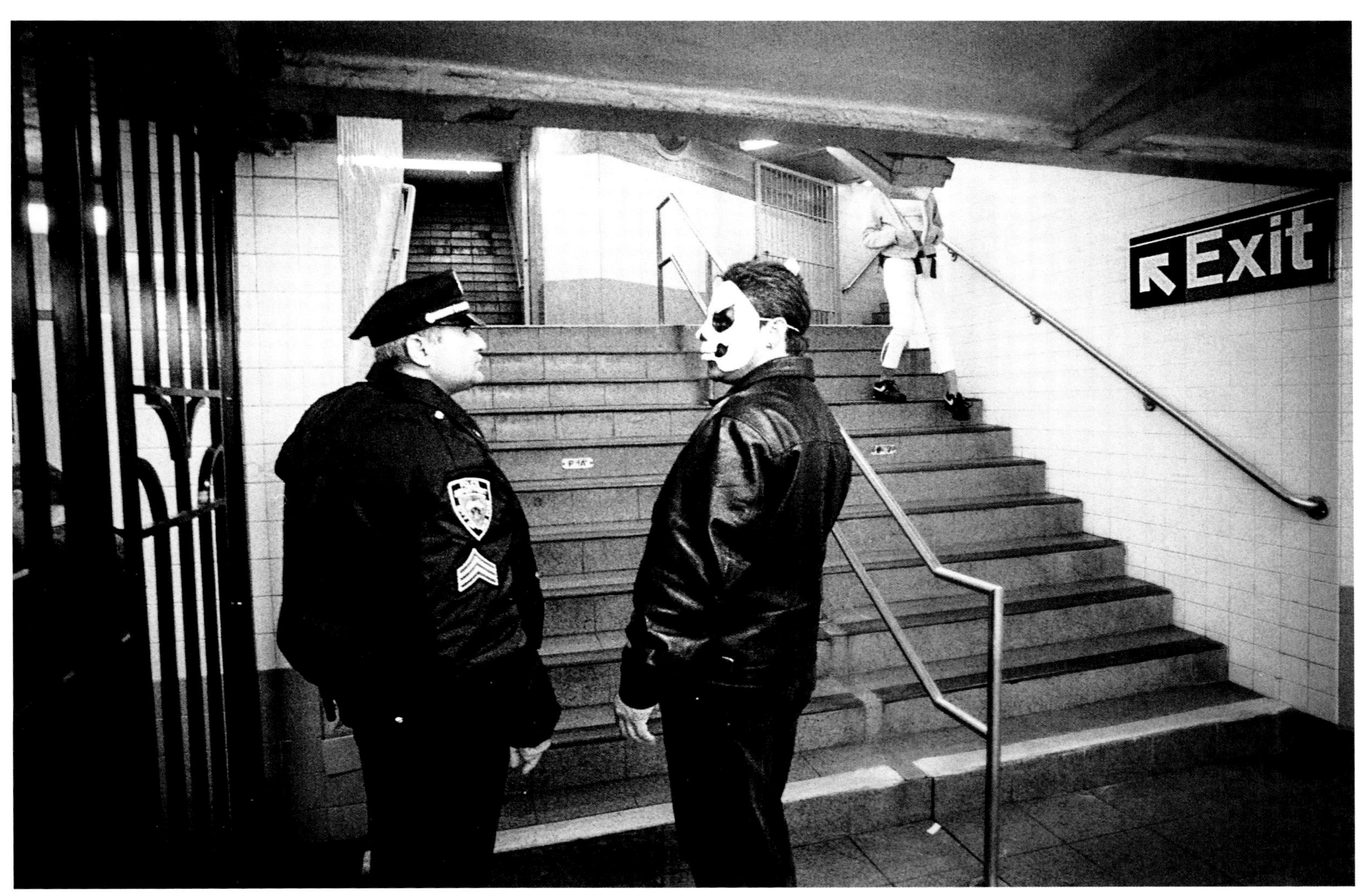

Exit

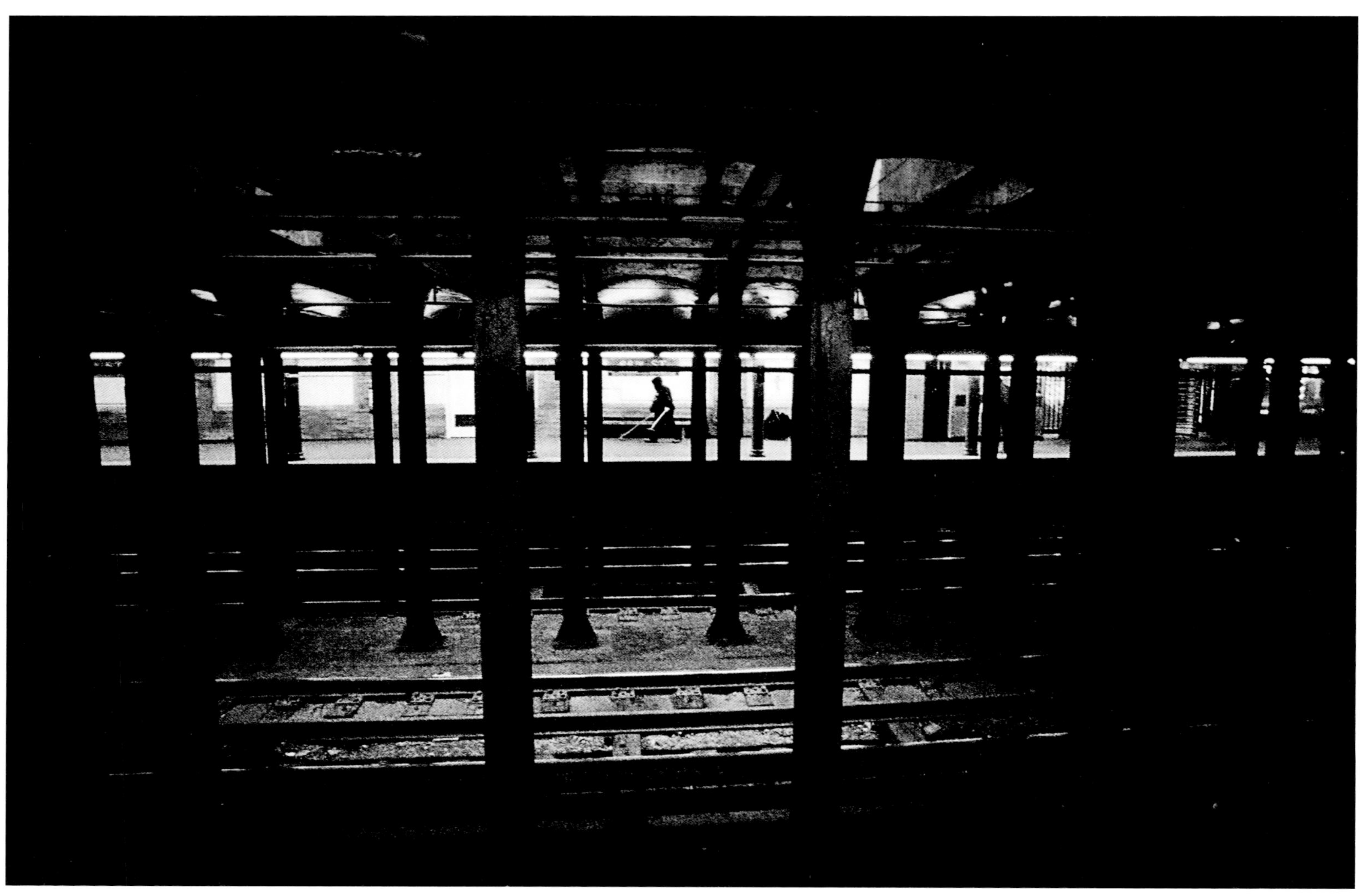

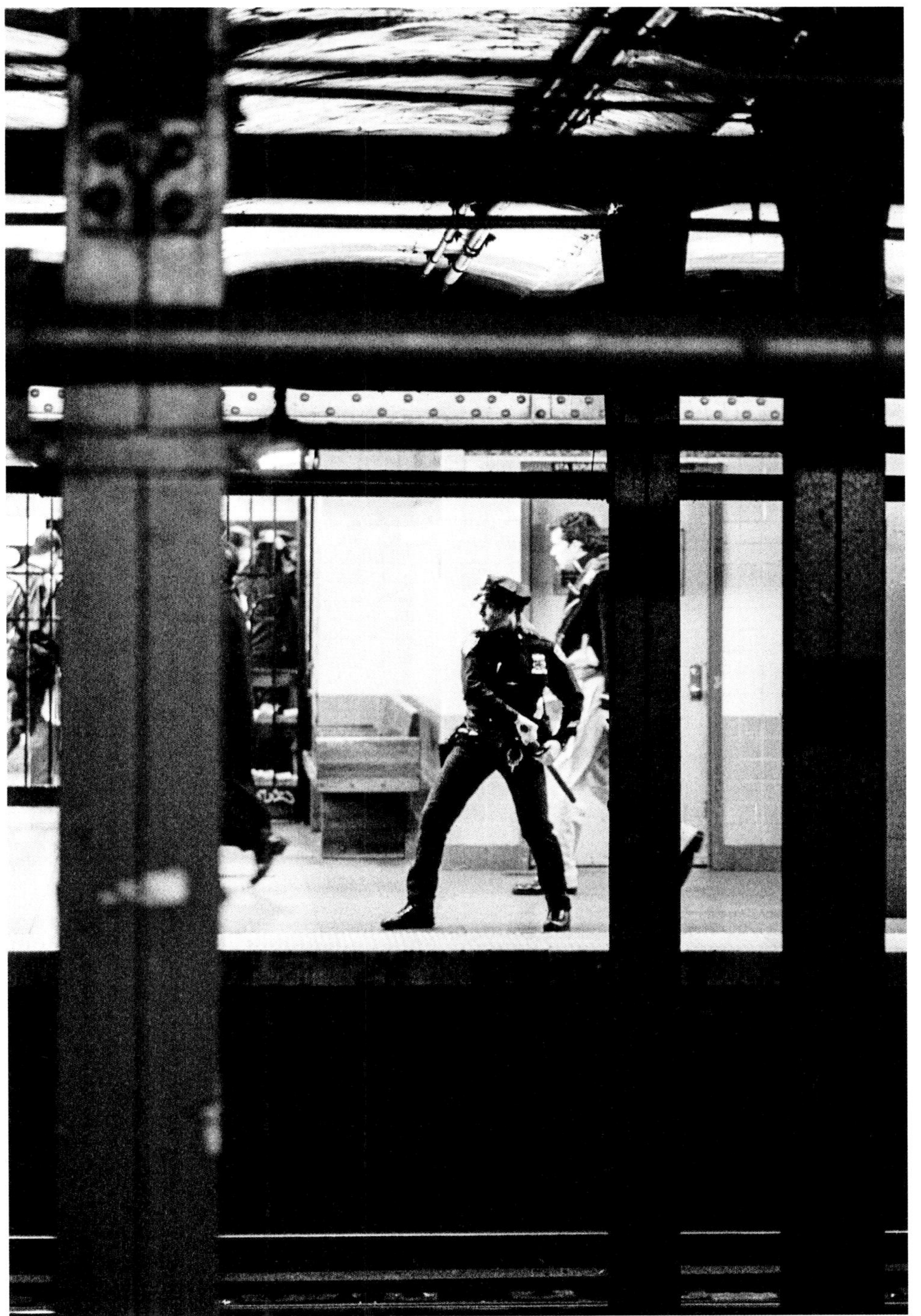

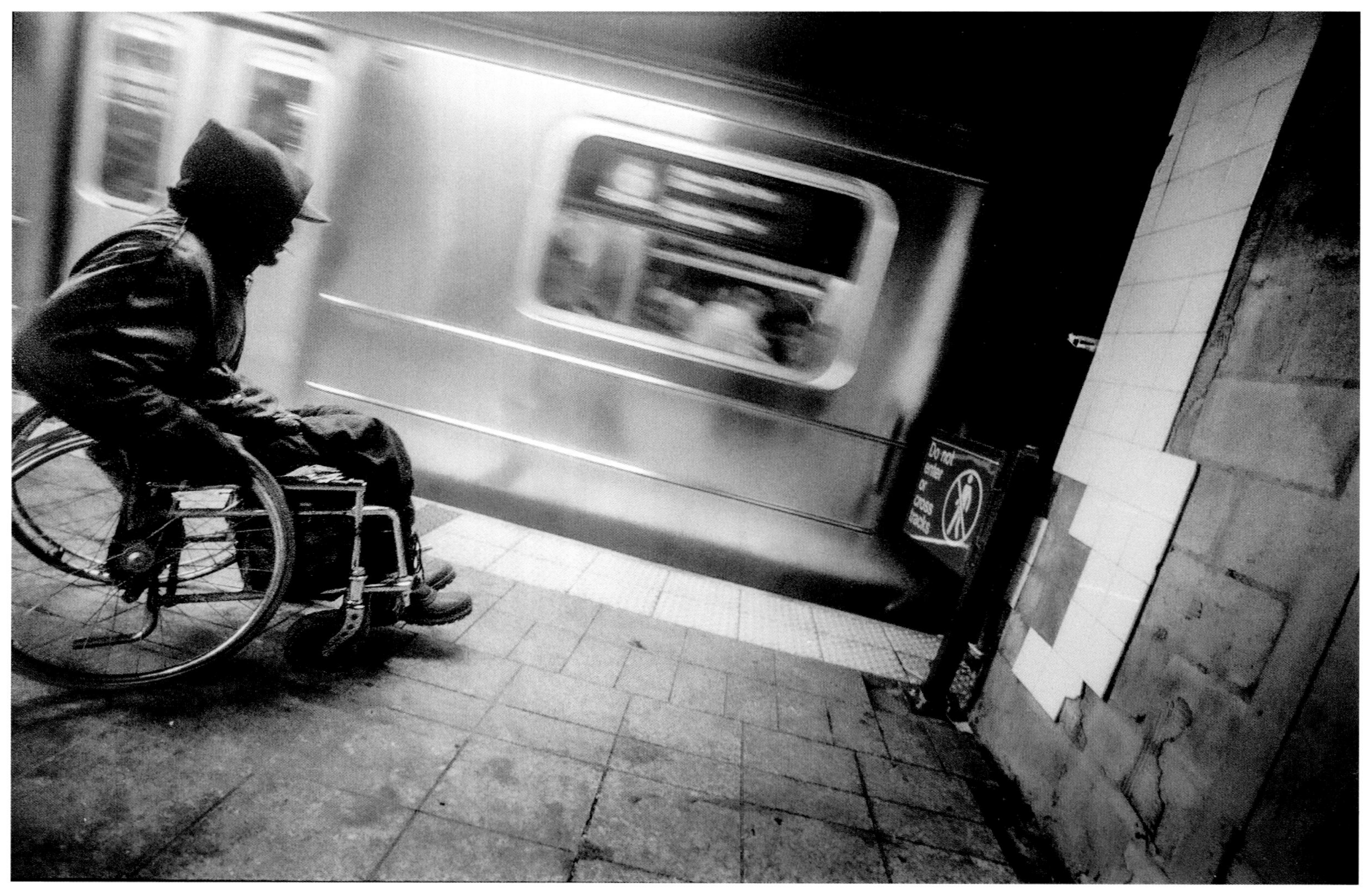

Do not
enter
or
cross
tracks

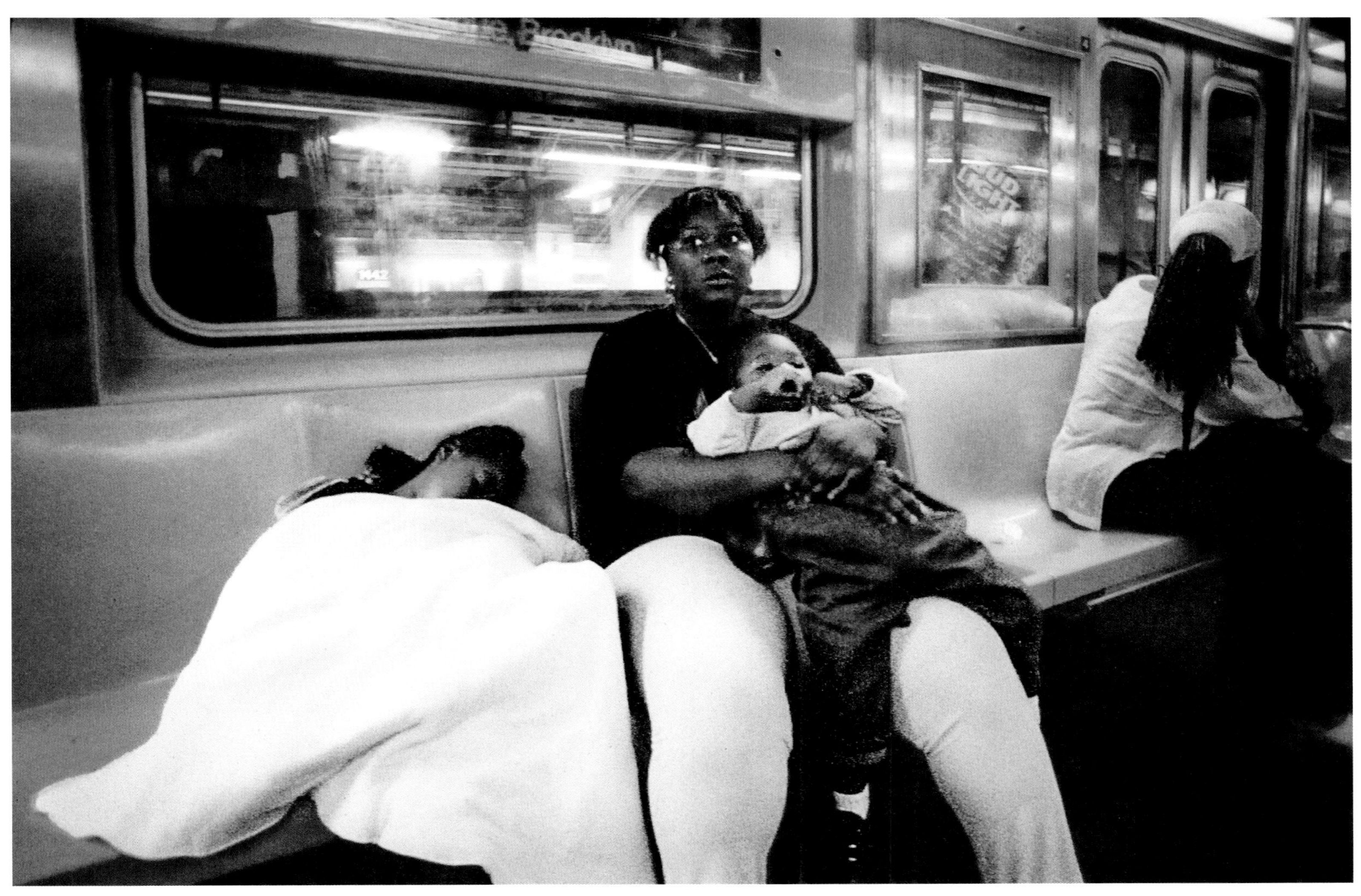

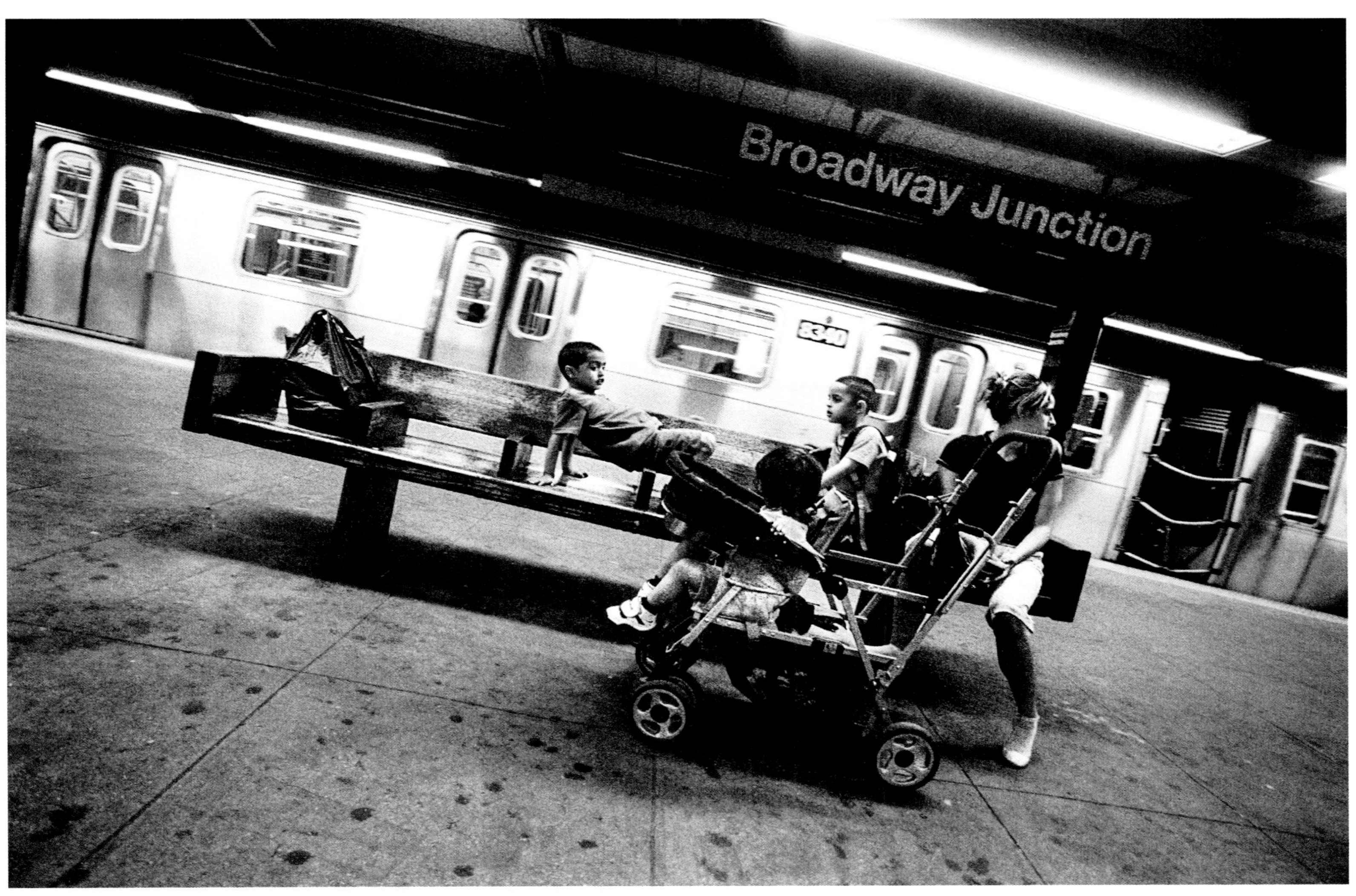

Broadway Junction

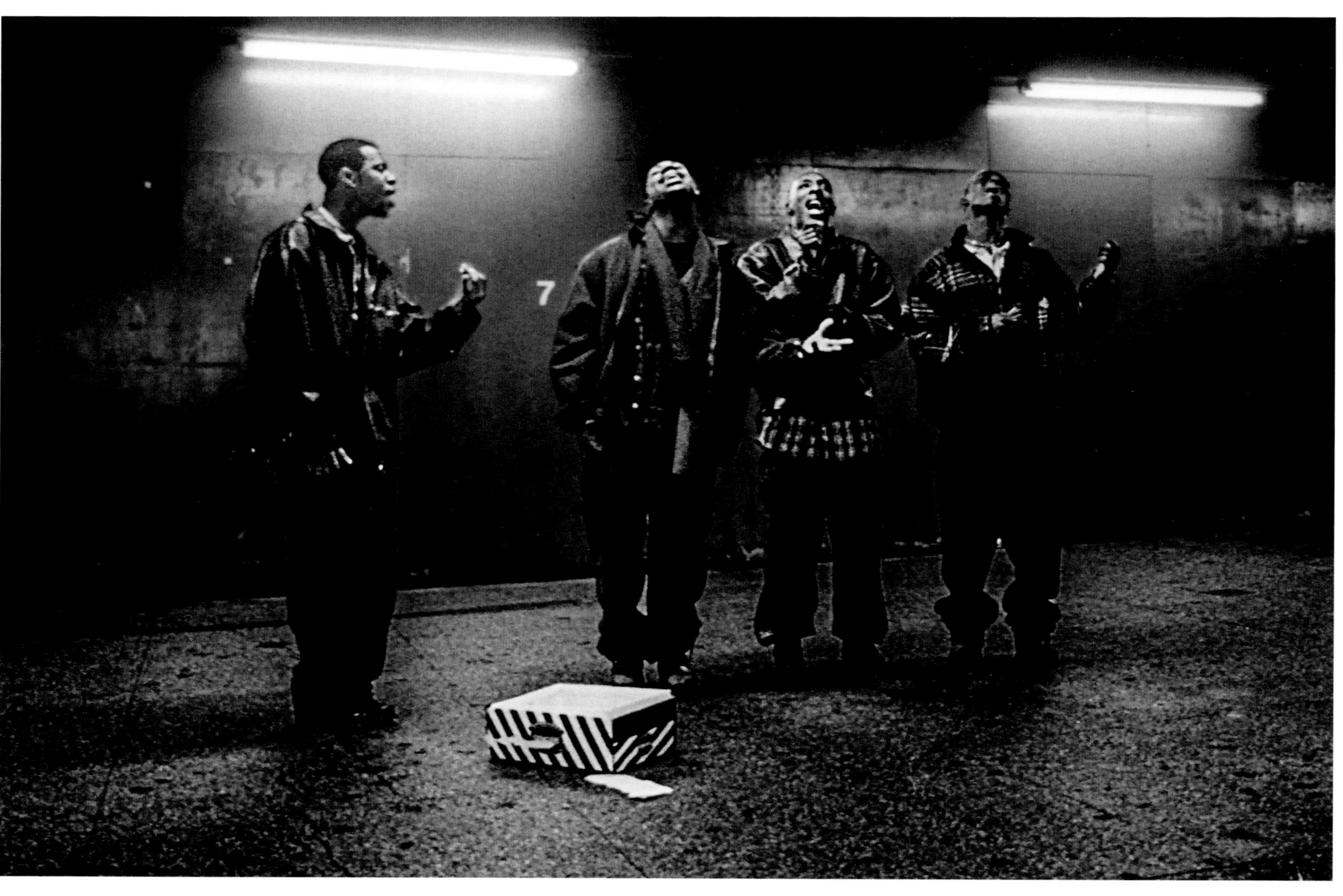

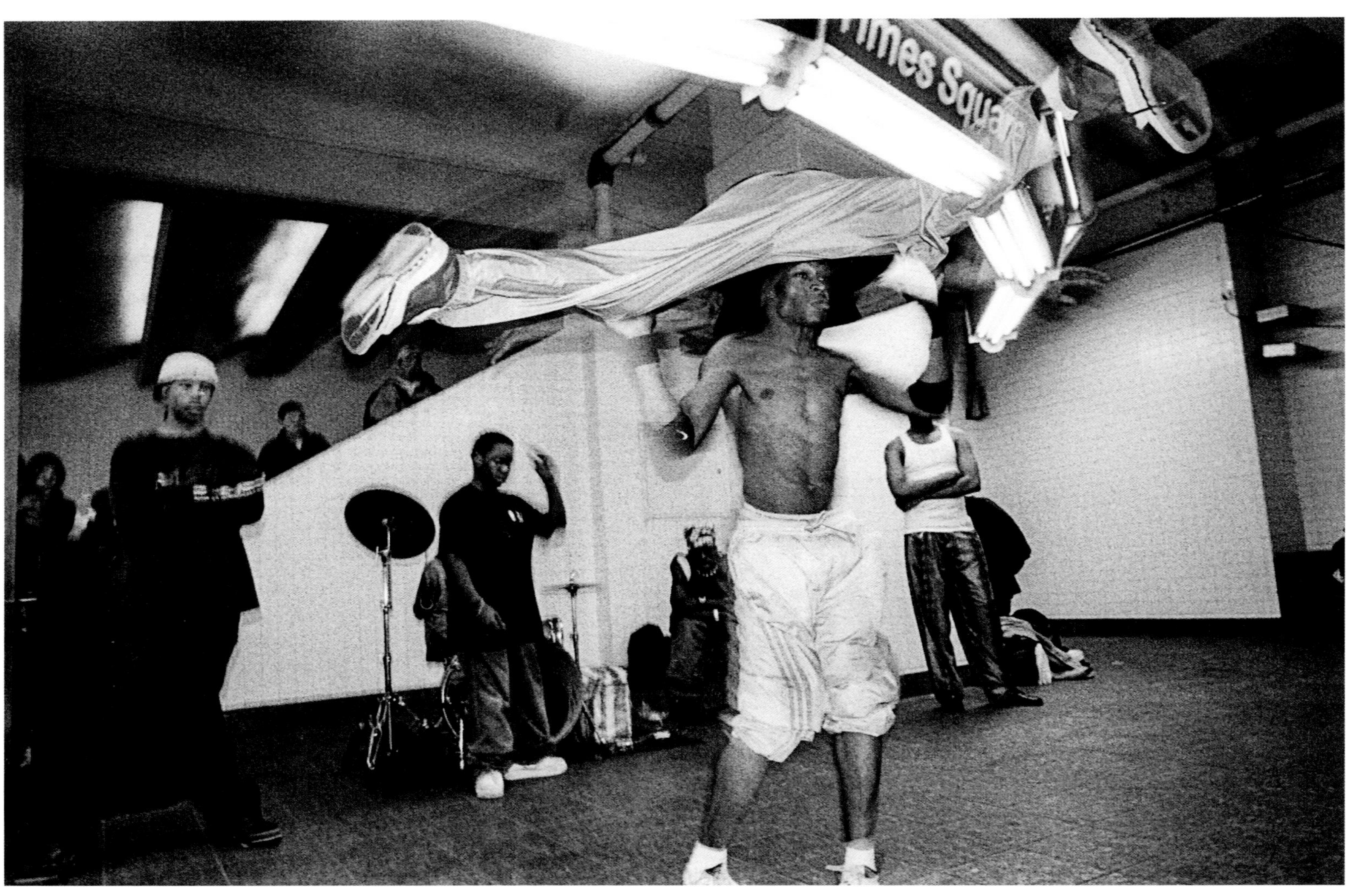

imes Square

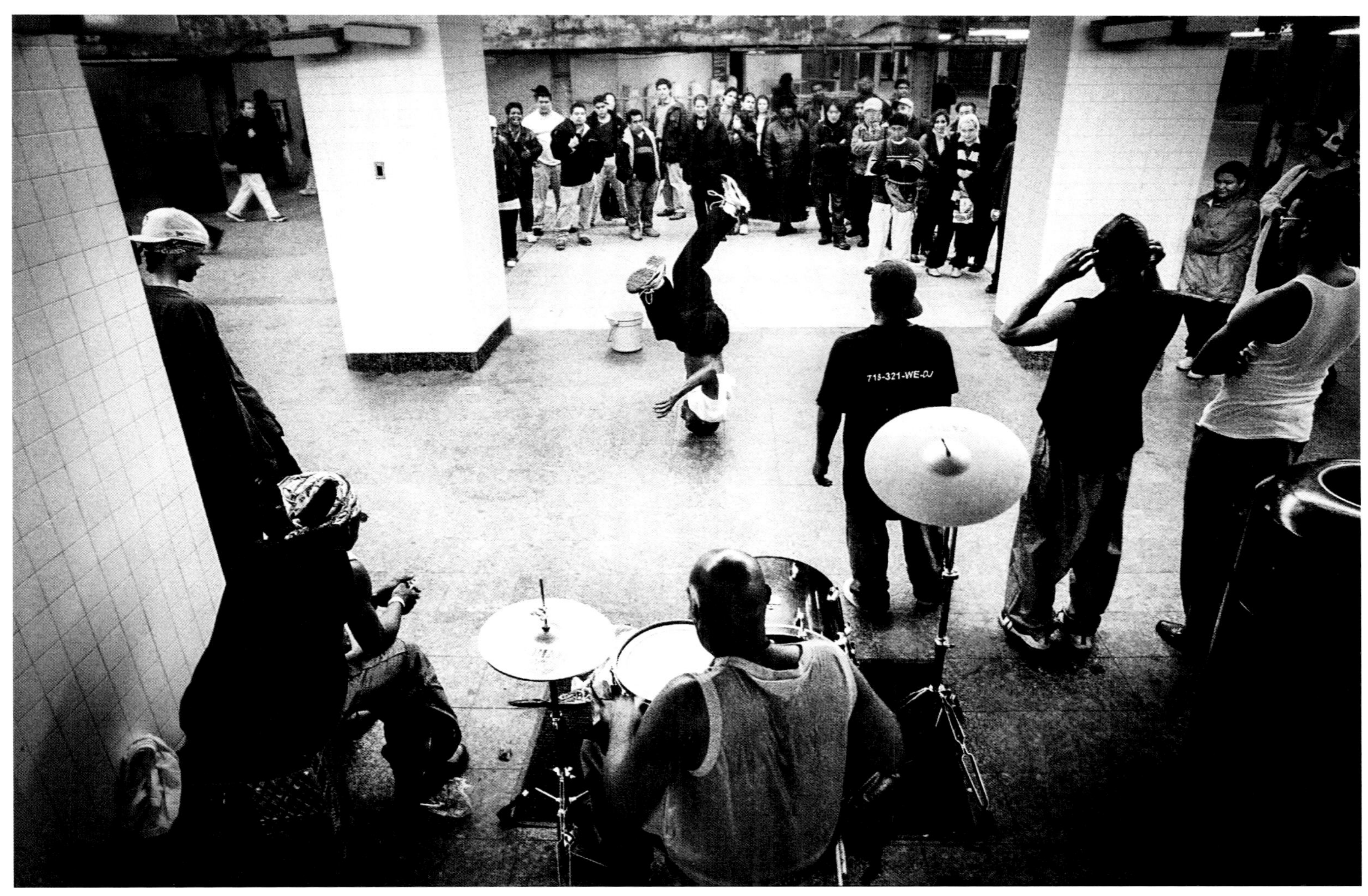

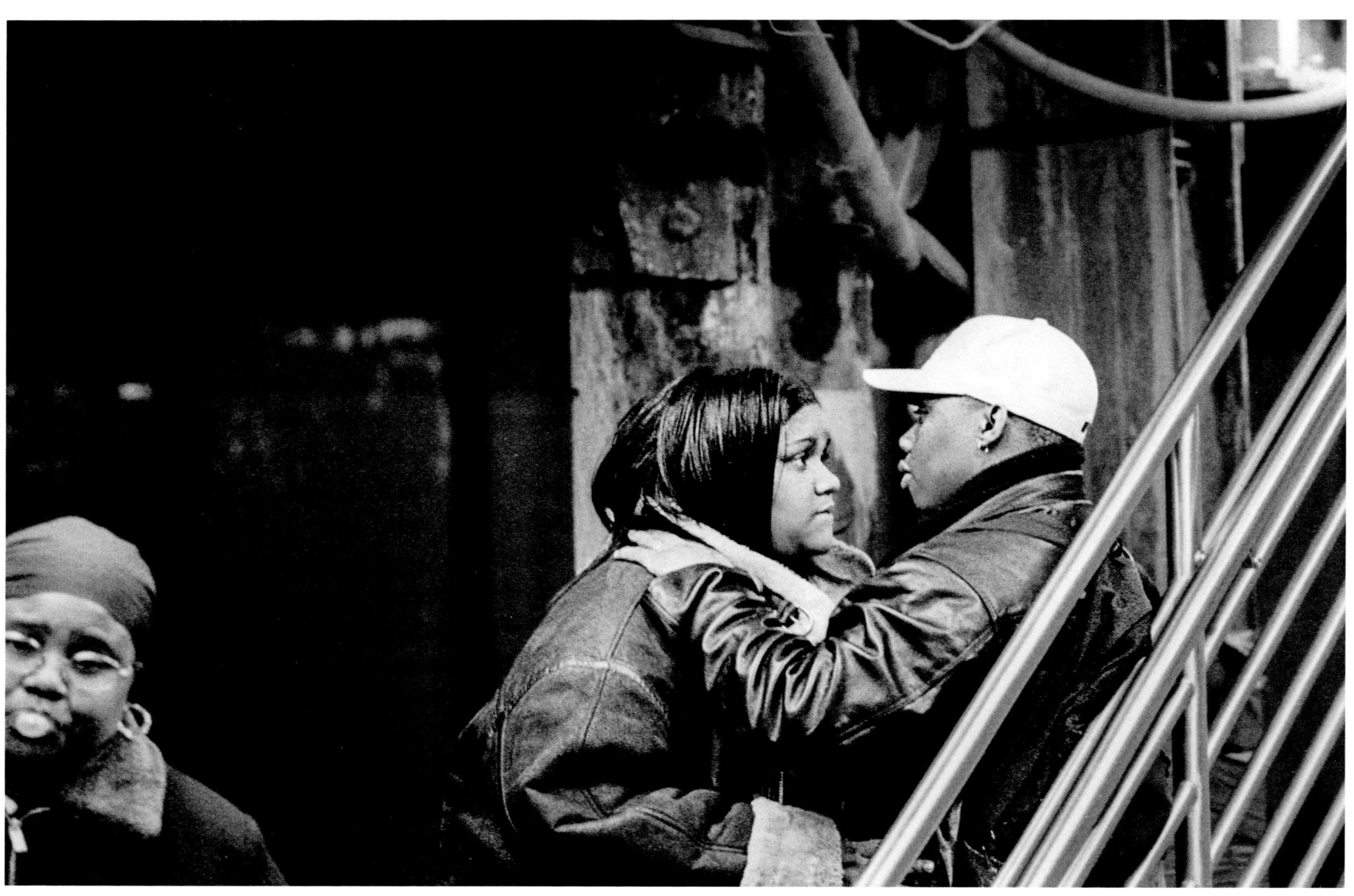

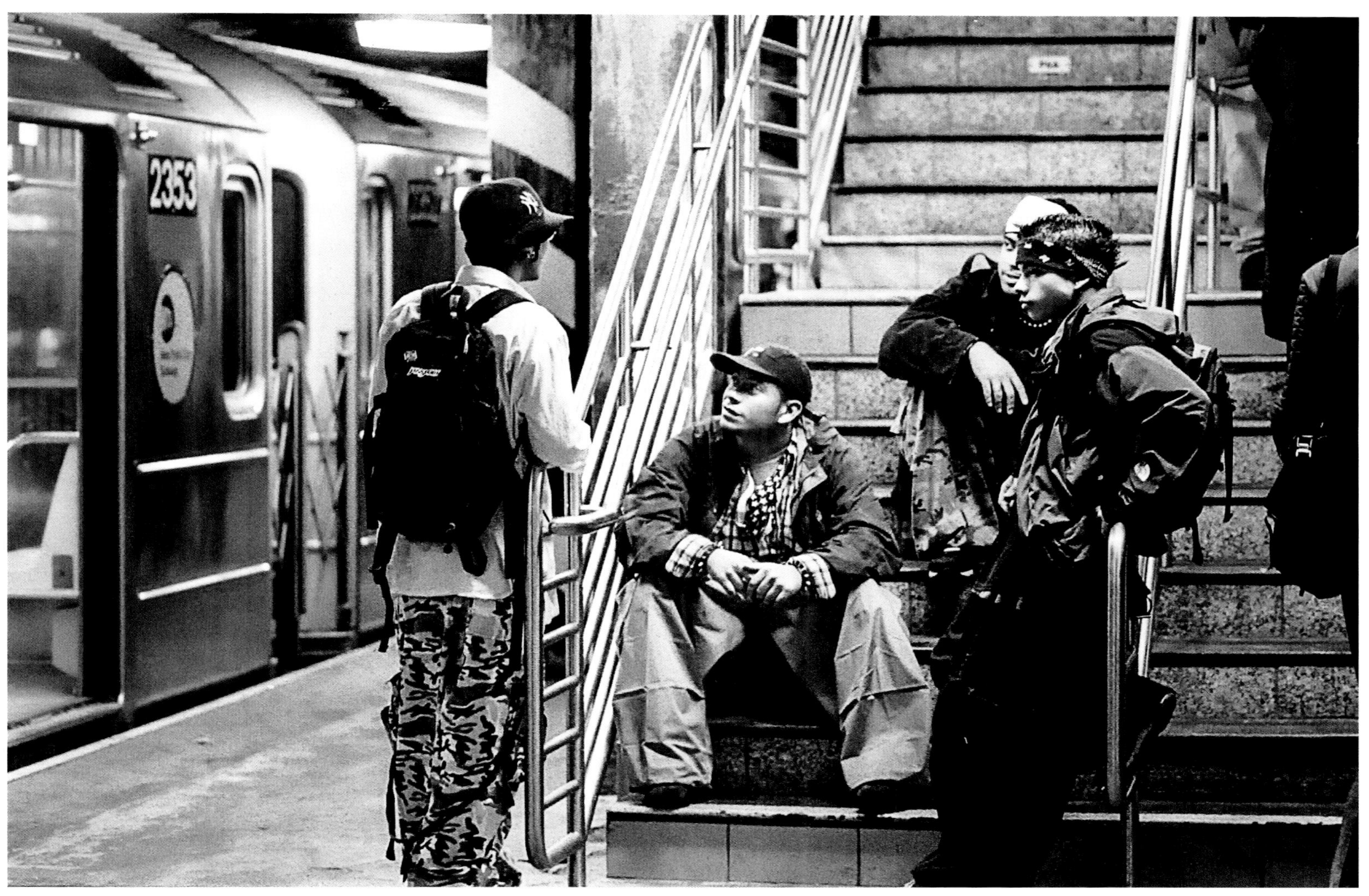

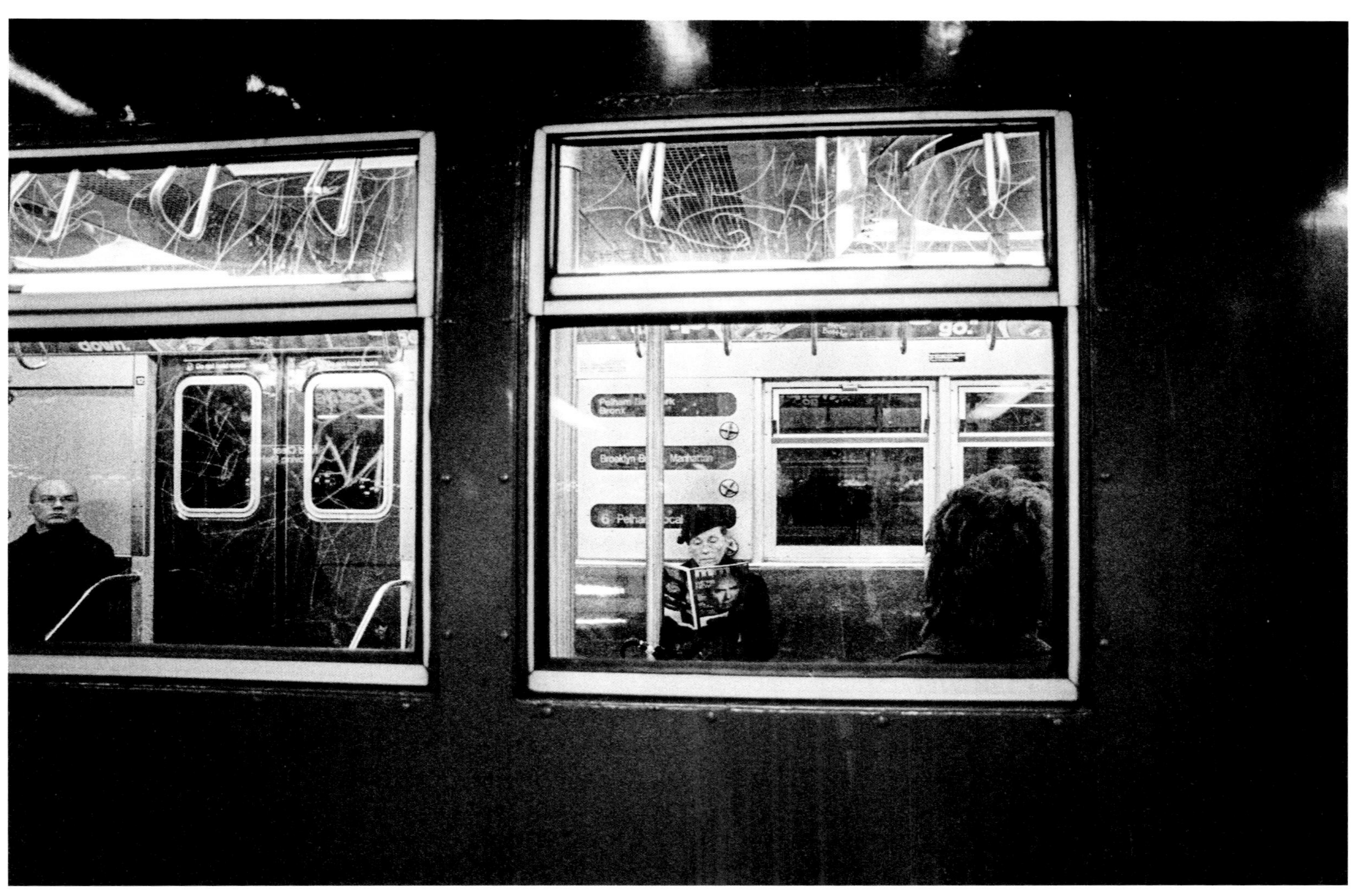

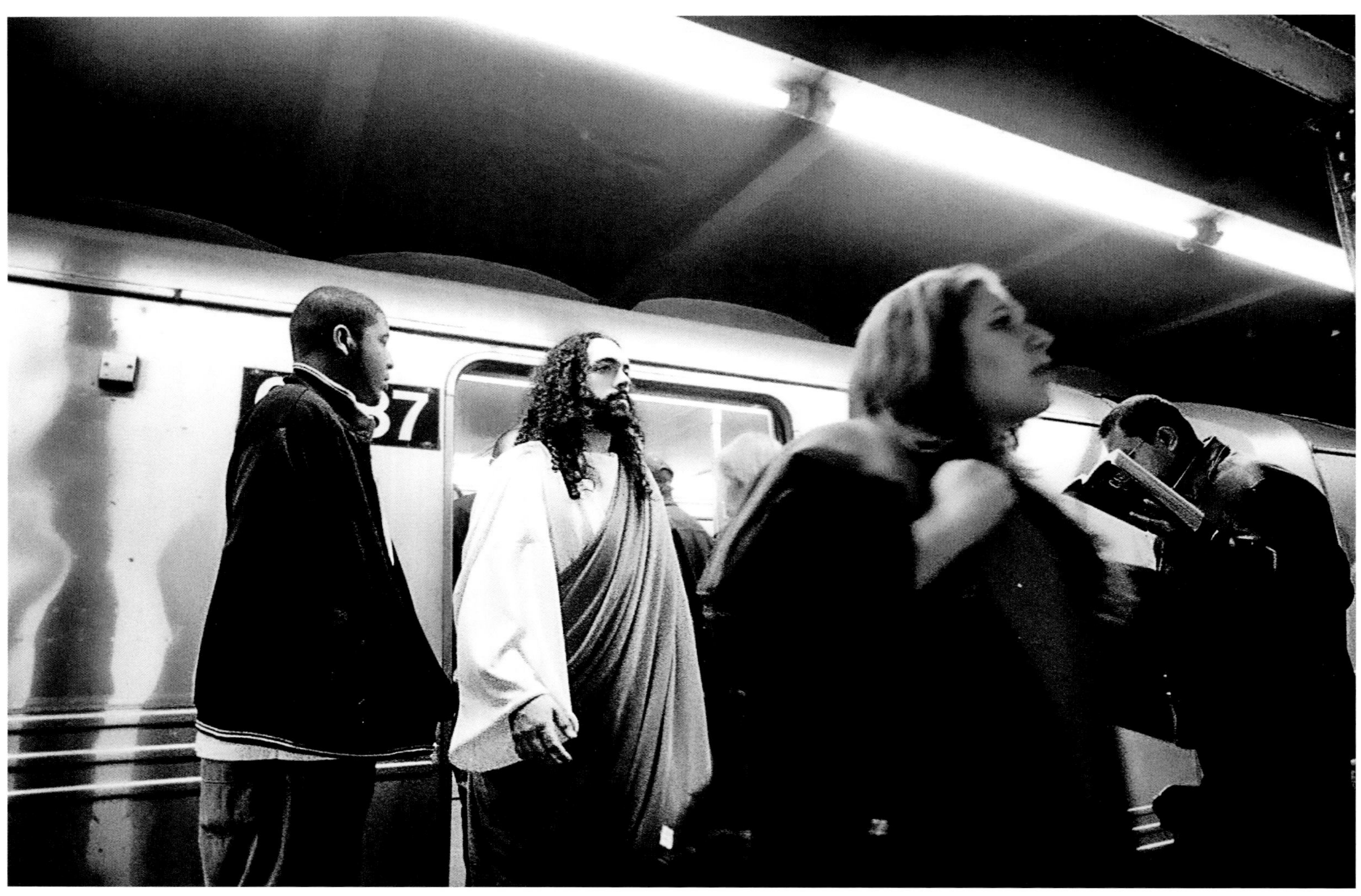

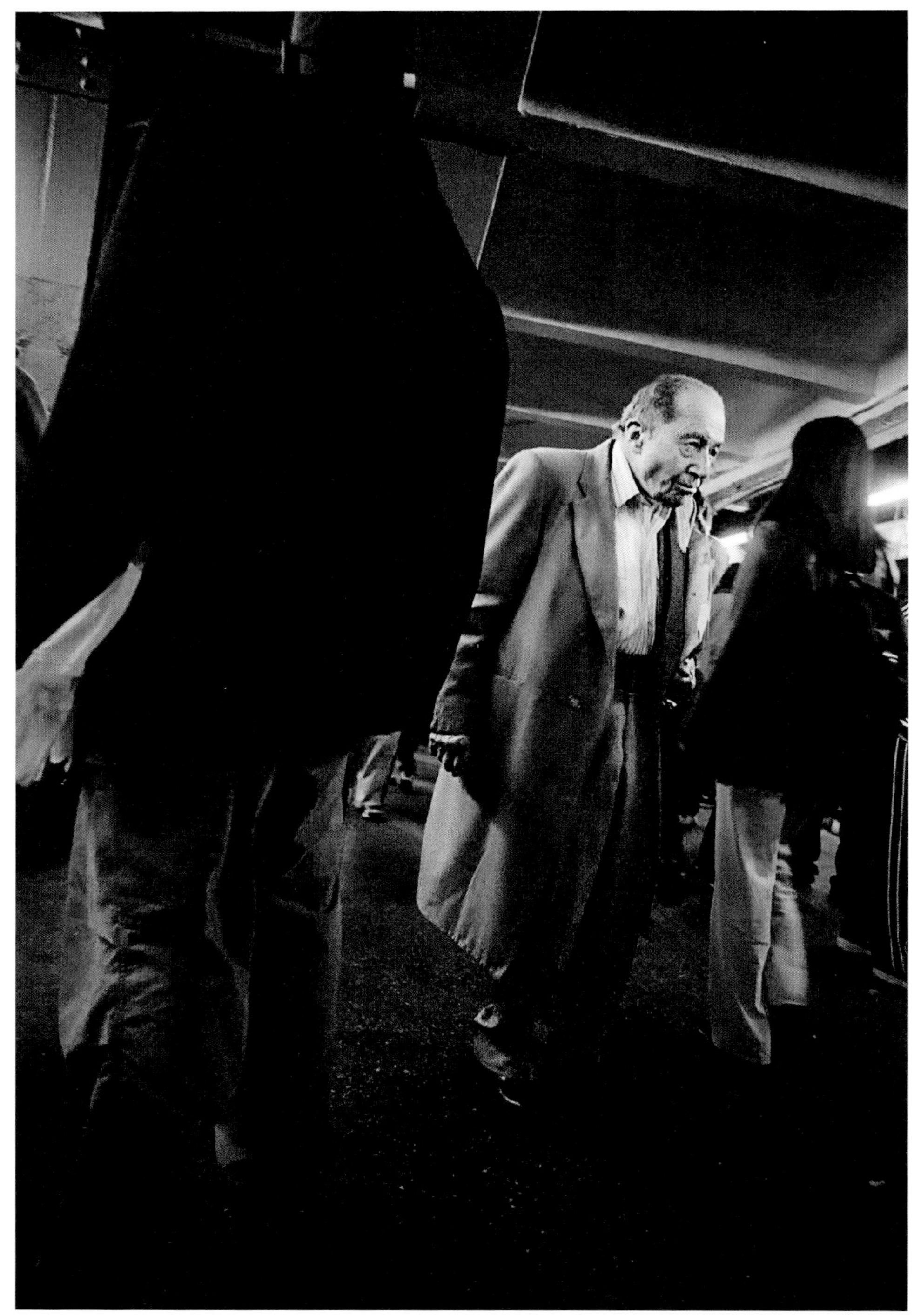

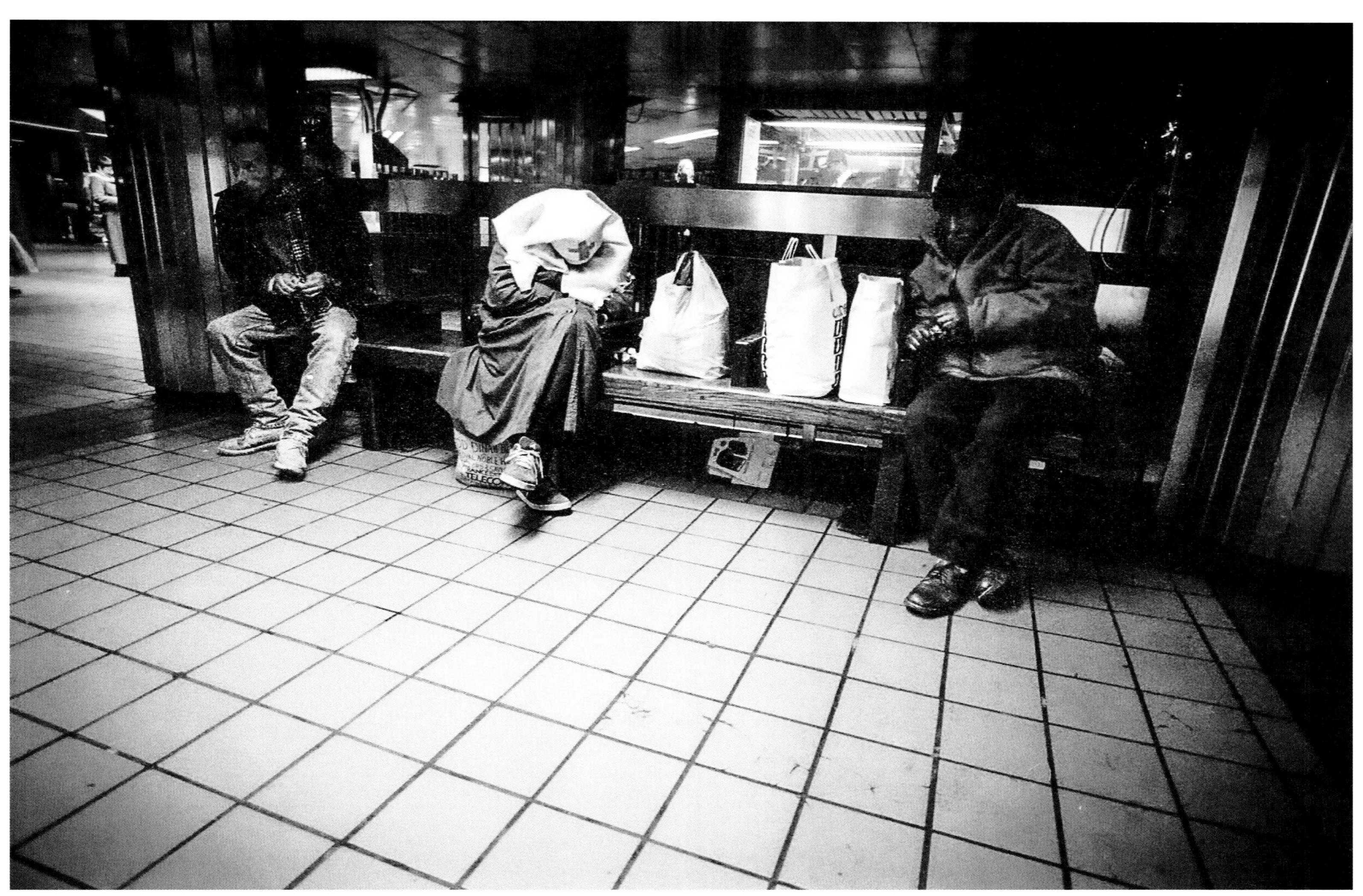

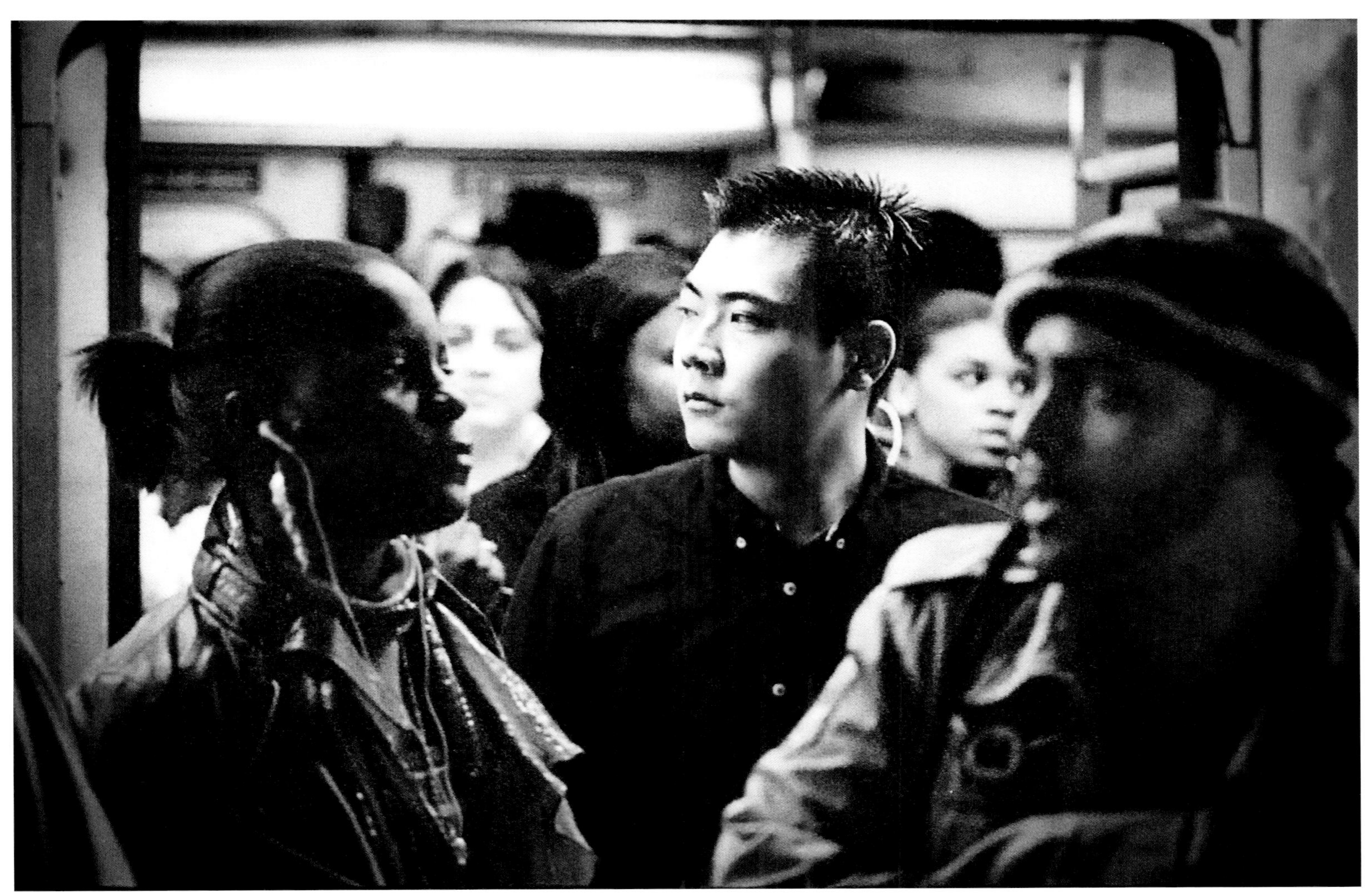

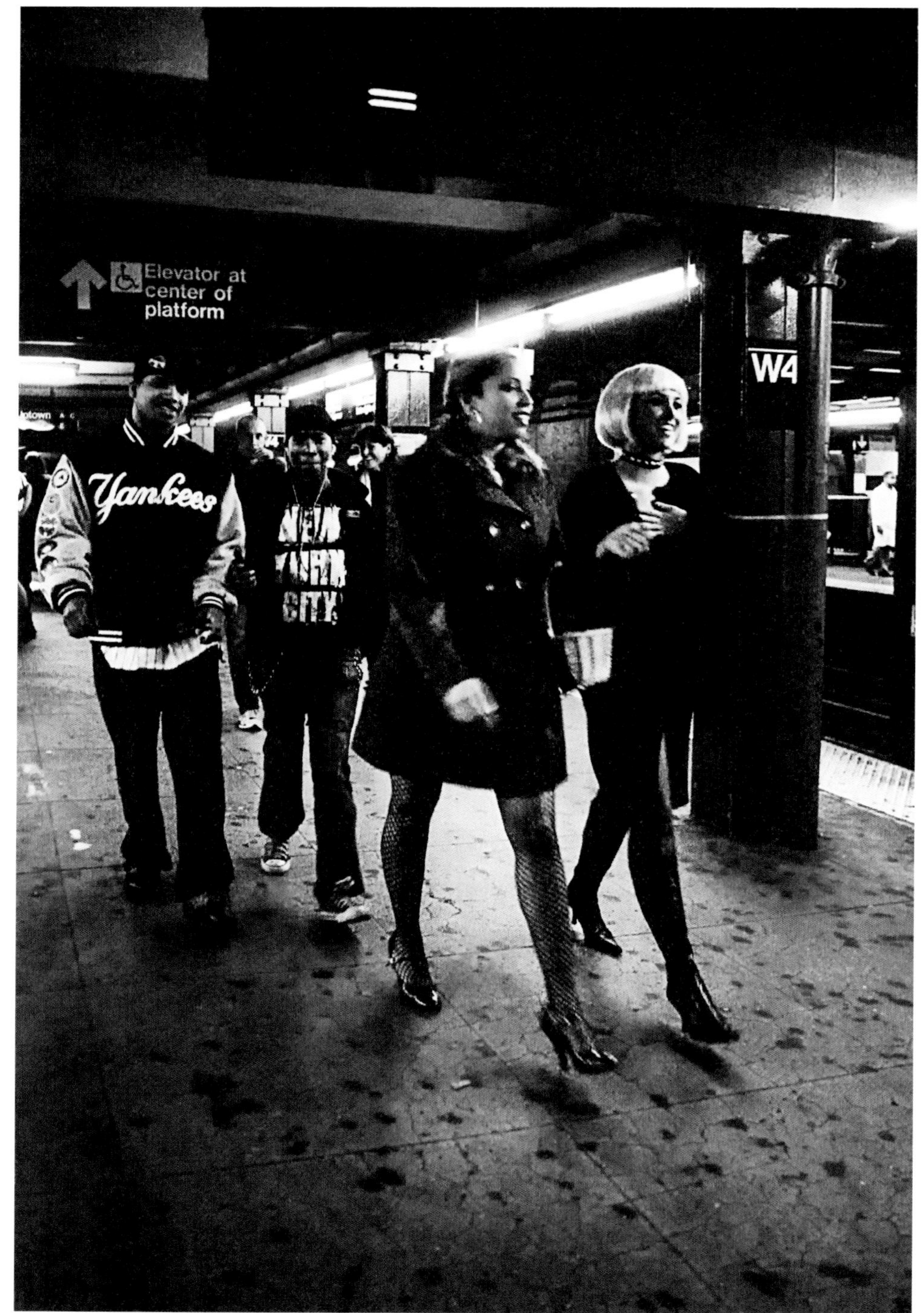

Elevator at
center of
platform
Uptown A C
Yankees
NEW YORK CITY
W4

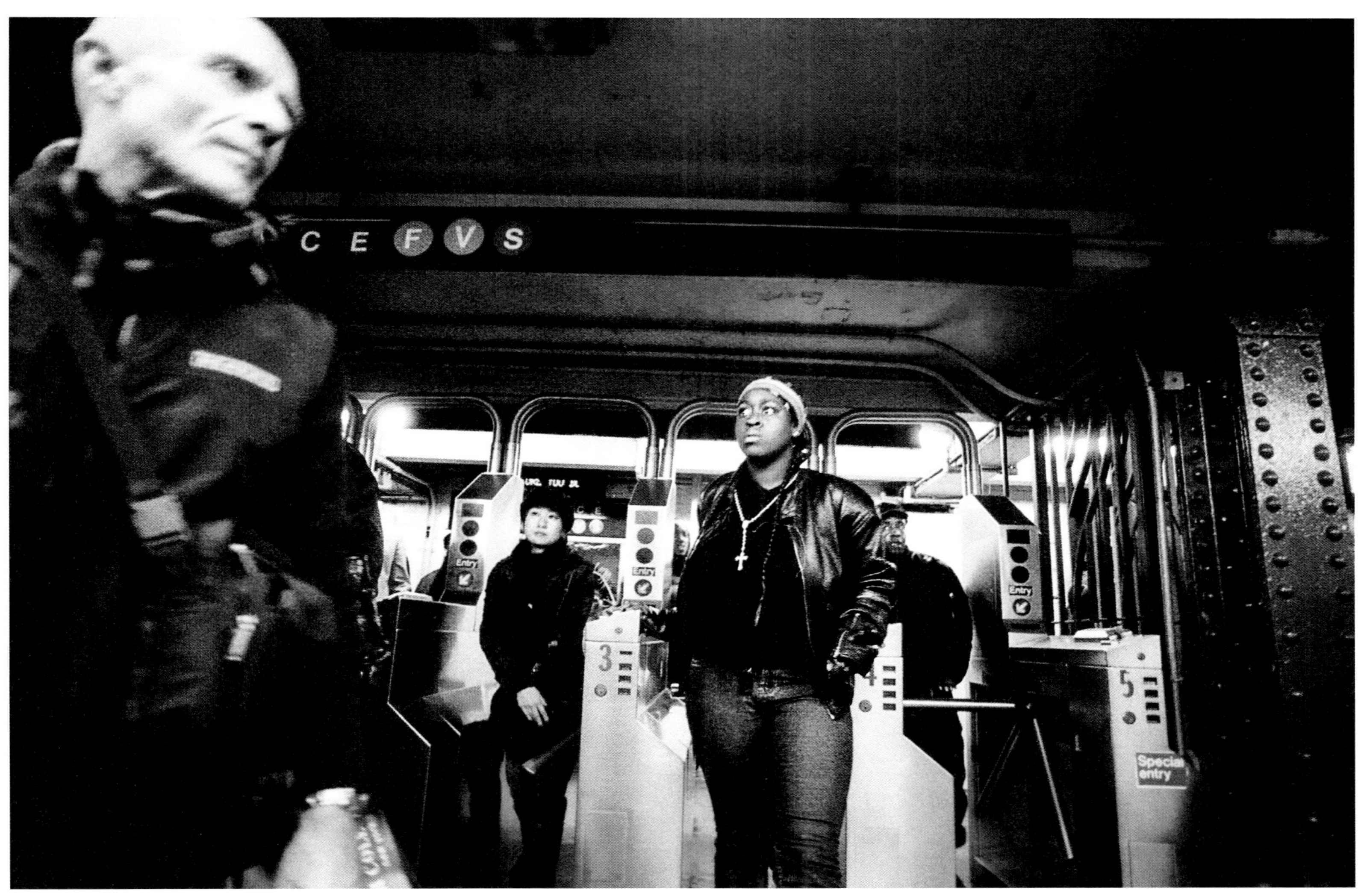
C E F V S
Entry
Entry
Entry
3
4
5
Special
entry

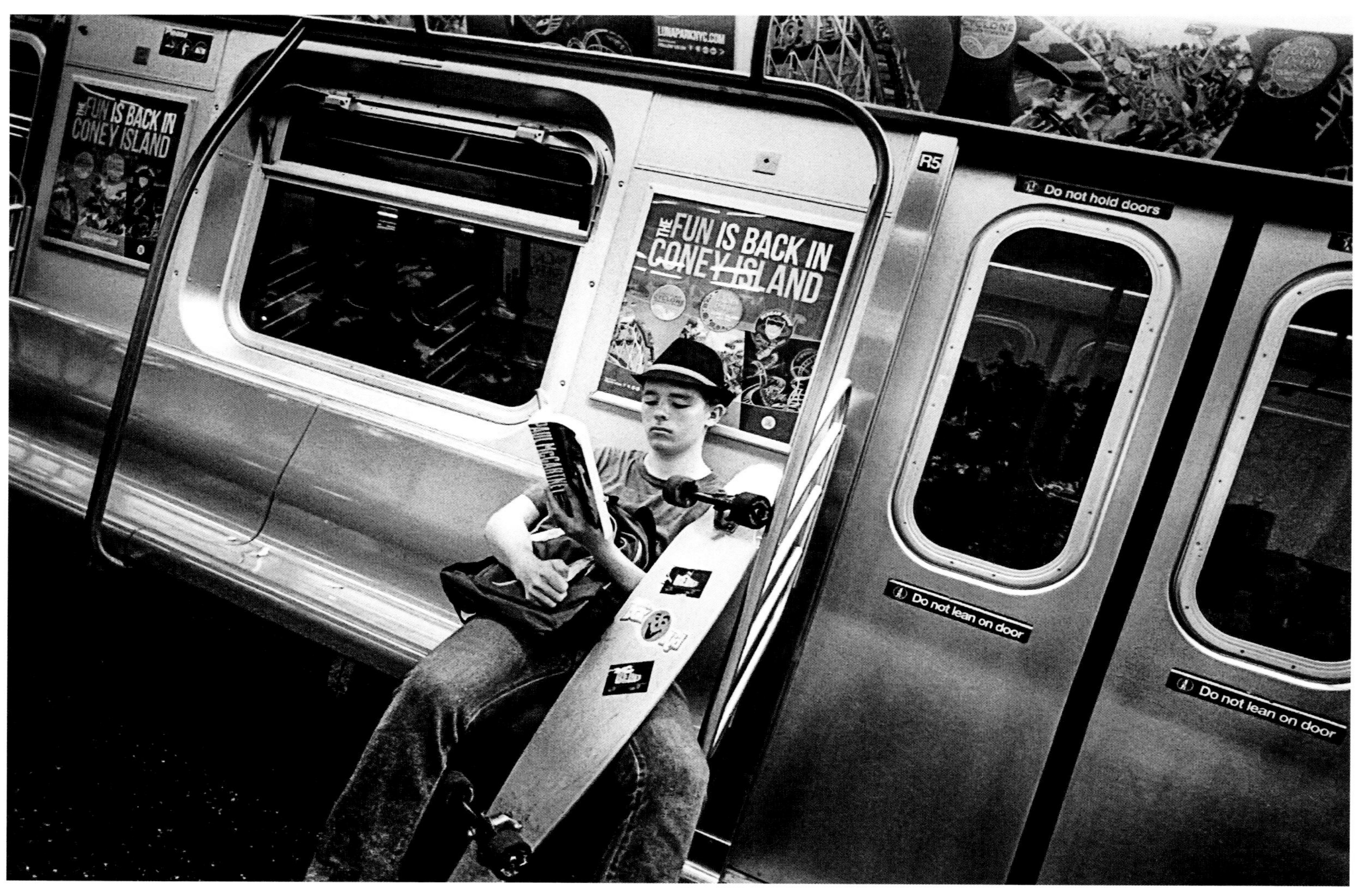

LUNAPARKNYC.COM
THE FUN IS BACK IN CONEY ISLAND
THE FUN IS BACK IN CONEY ISLAND
R5
Do not hold doors
Do not lean on door
Do not lean on door

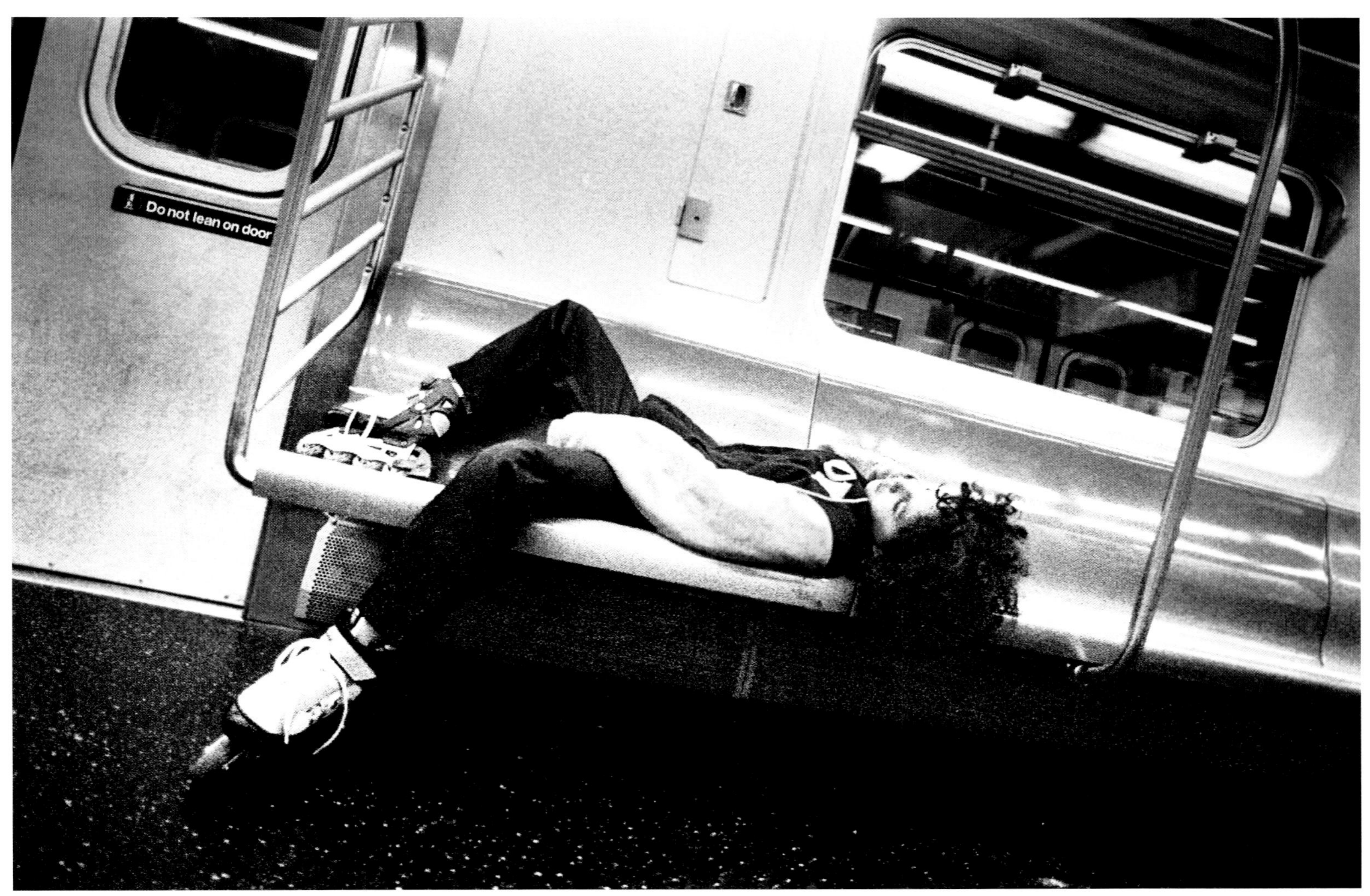
Do not lean on door

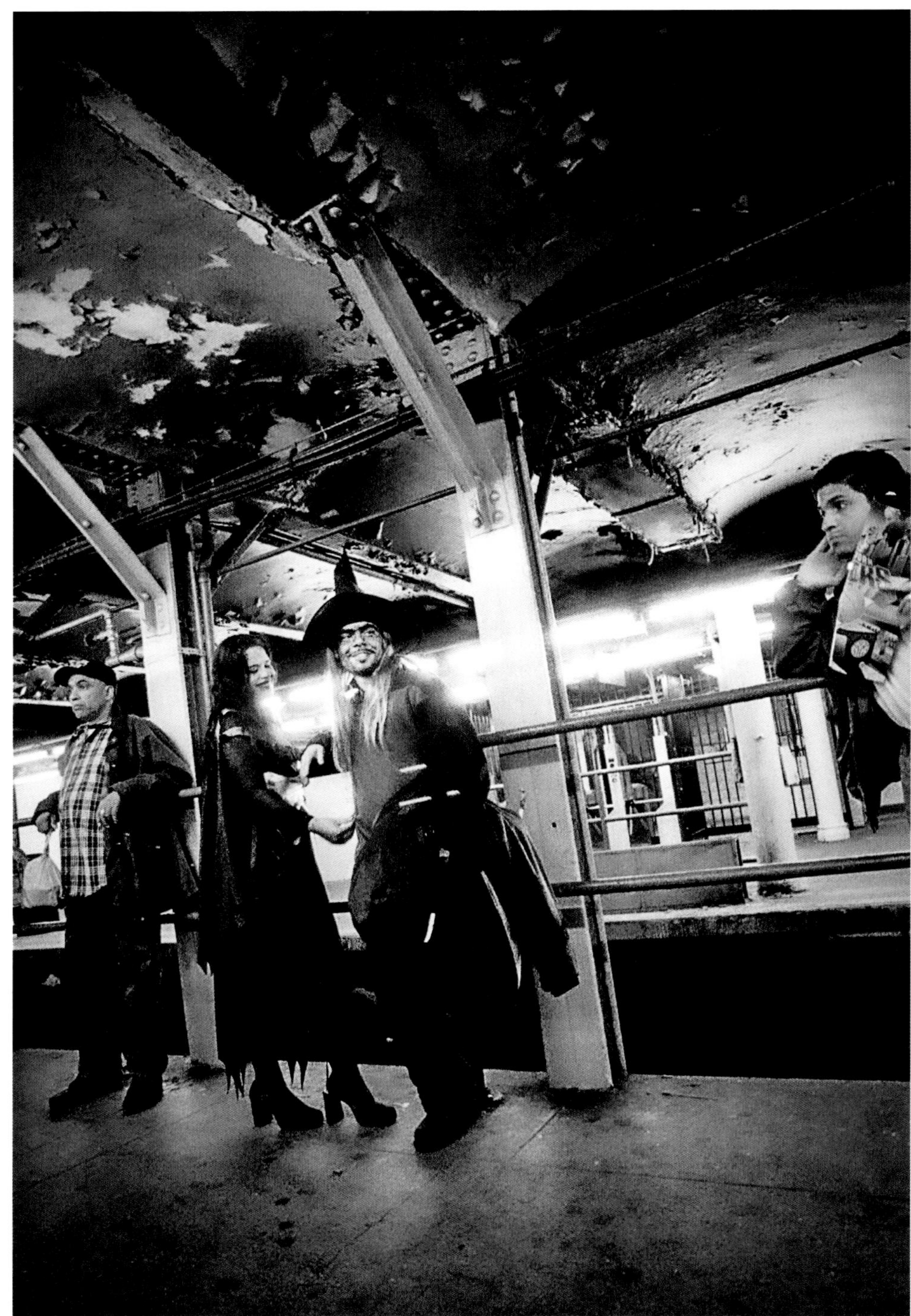

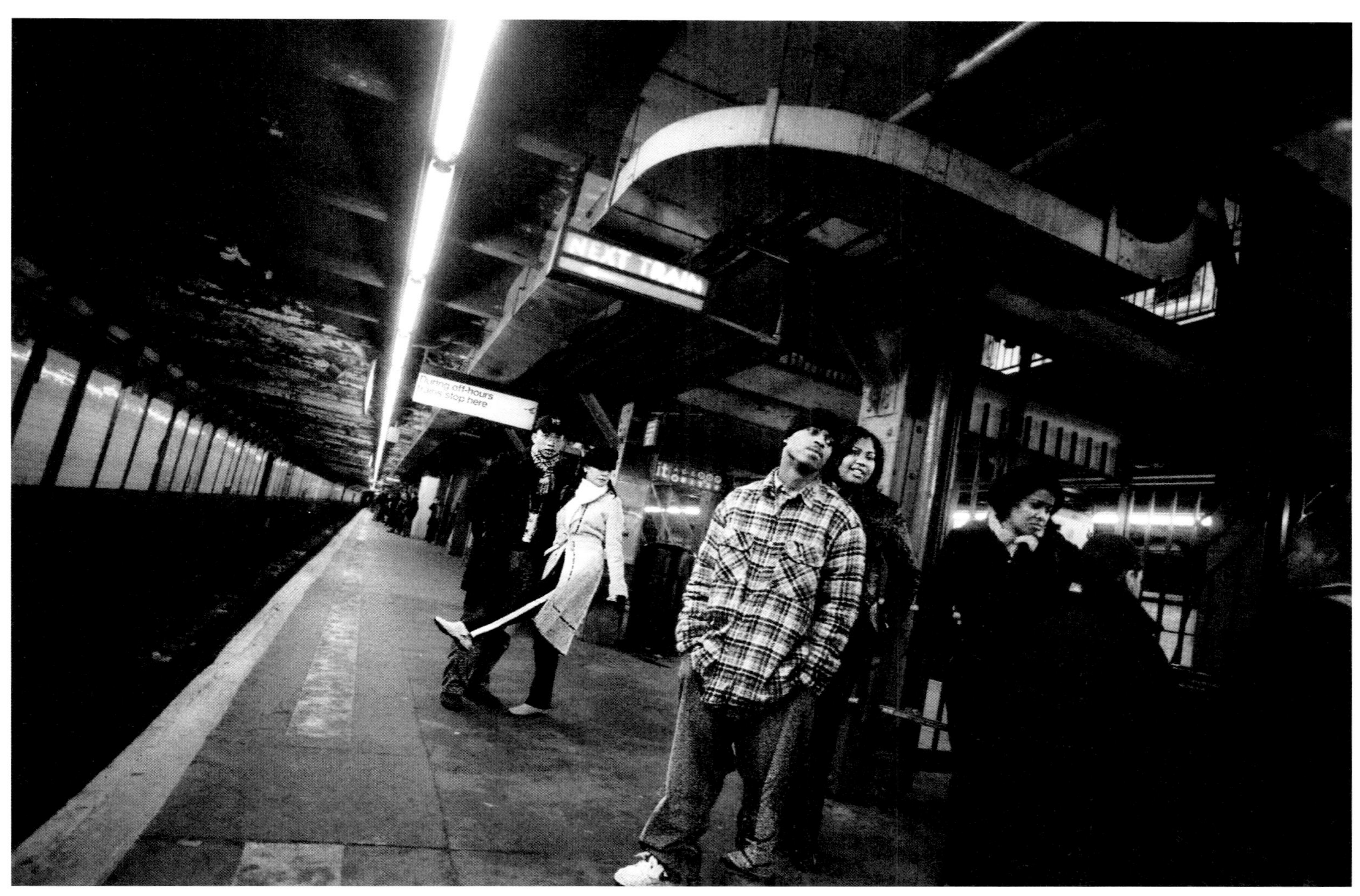
NEXT TRAIN
During off-hours
trains stop here

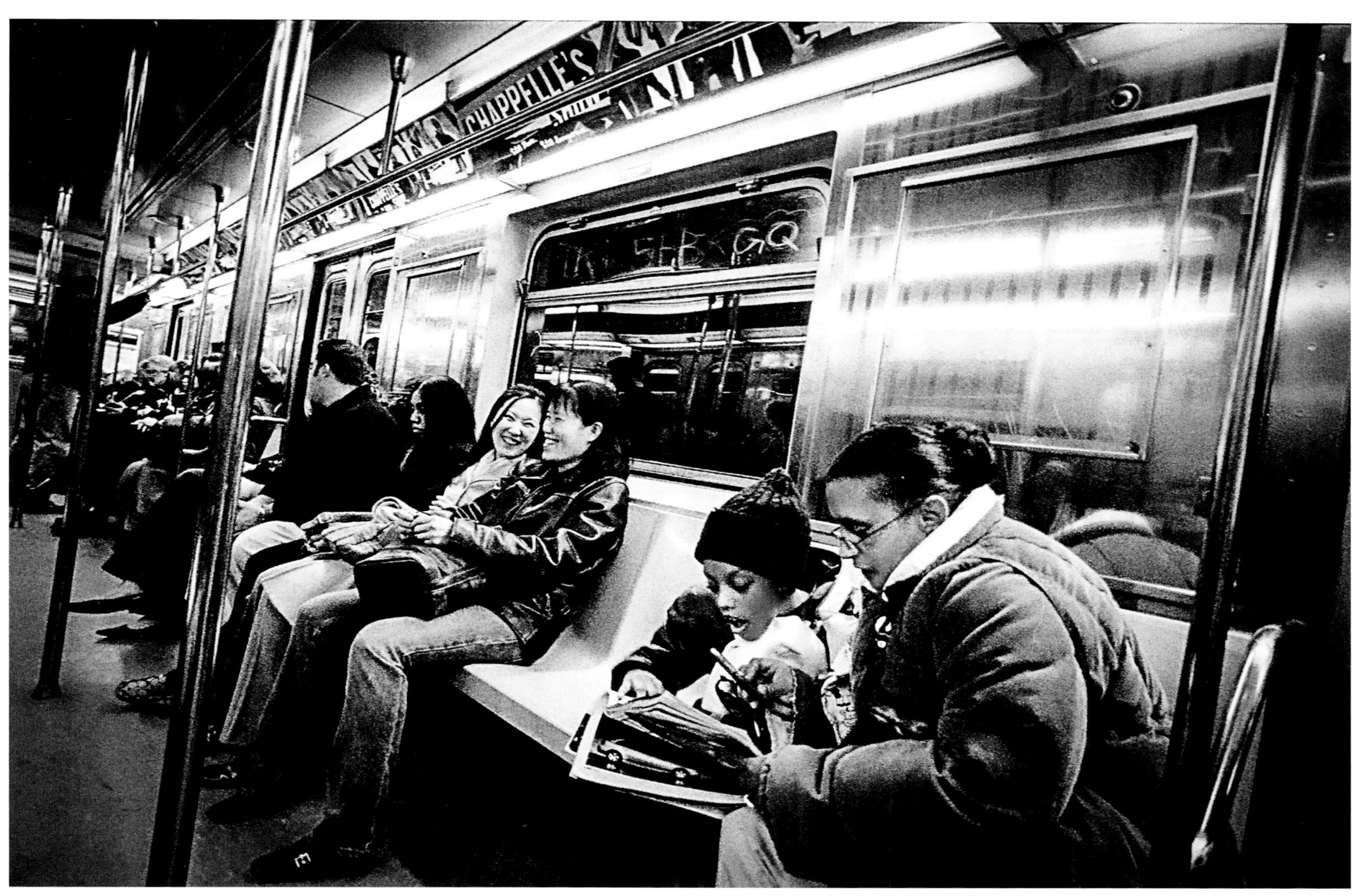

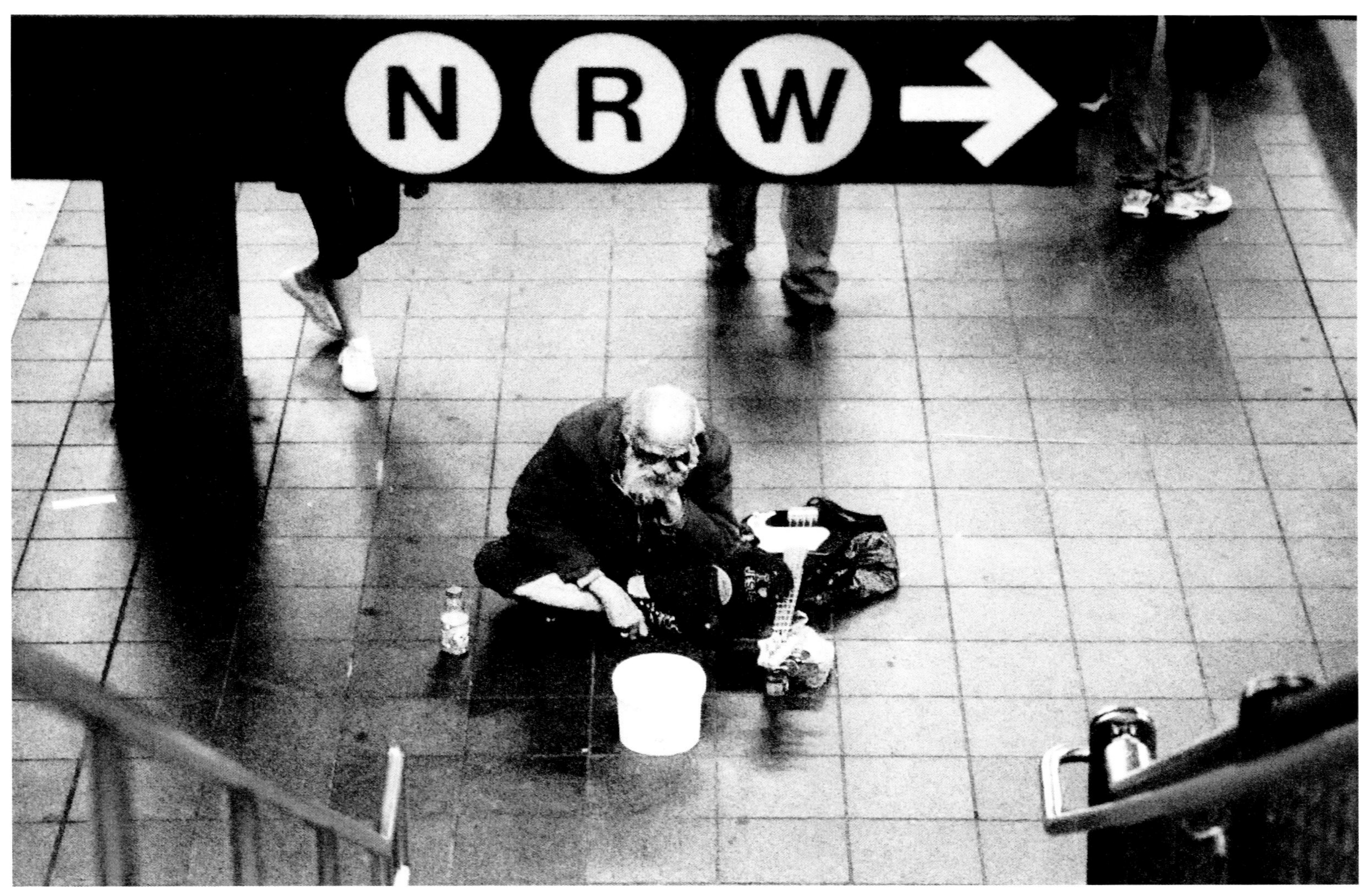

N R W →

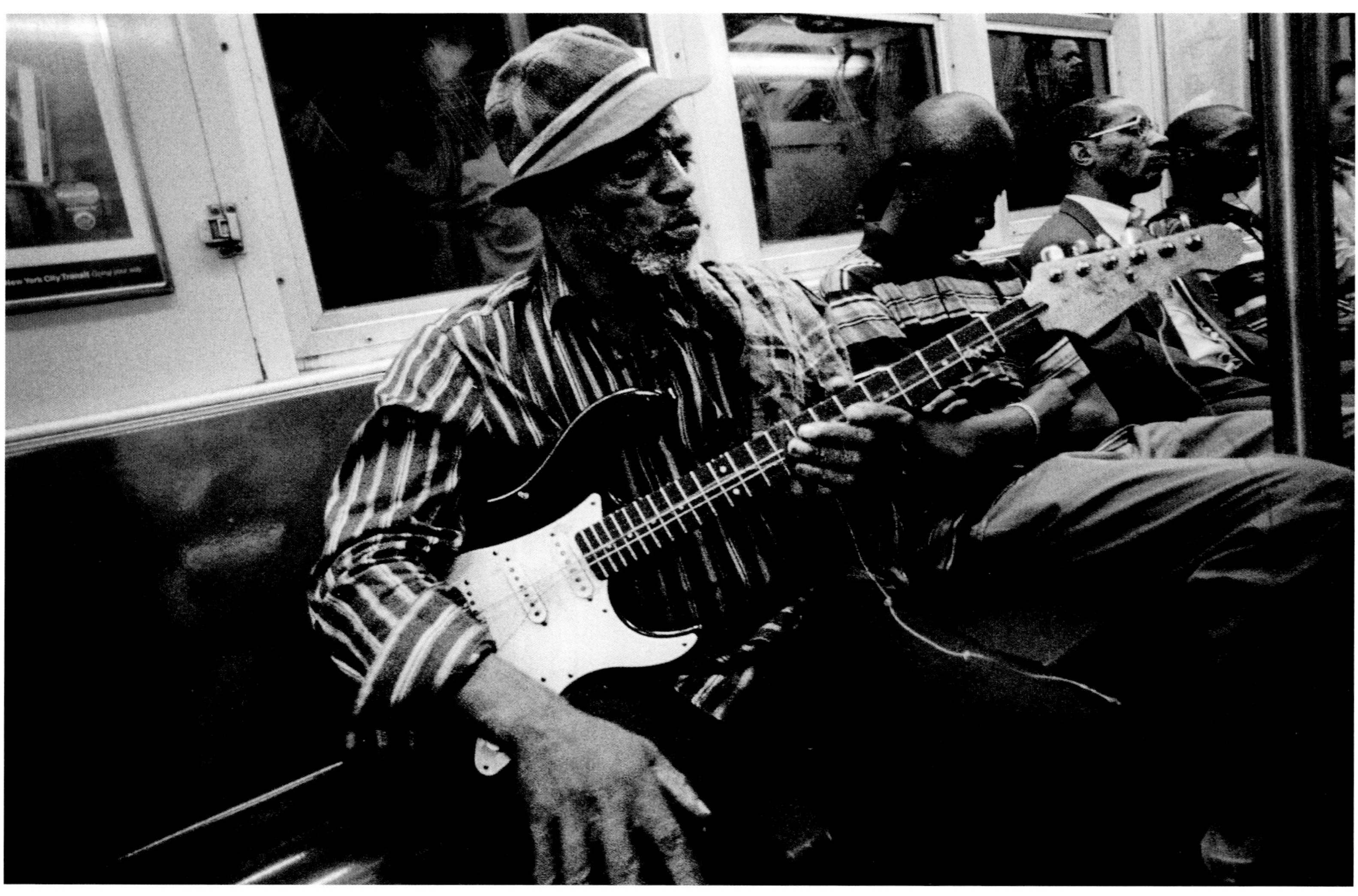

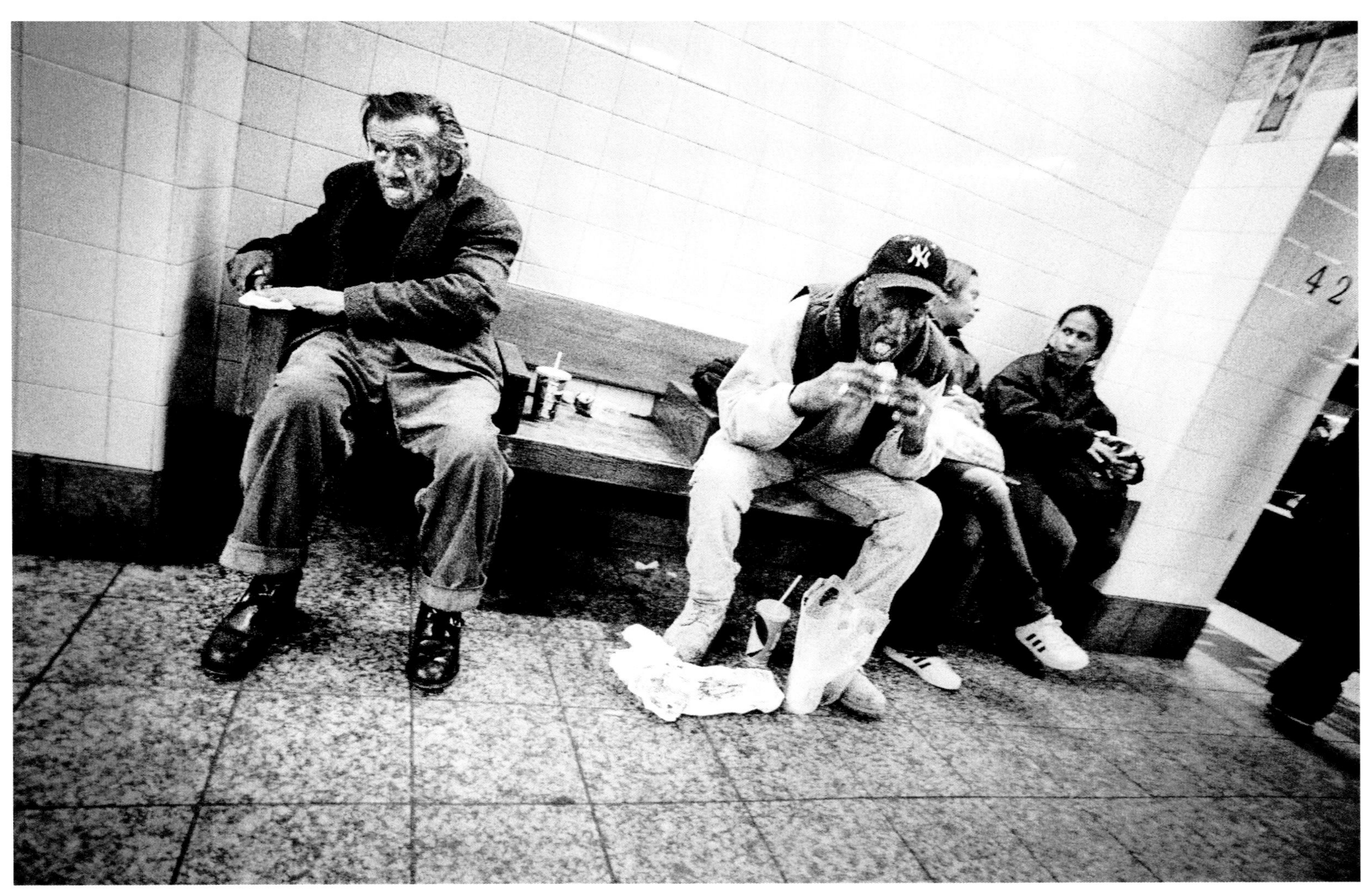

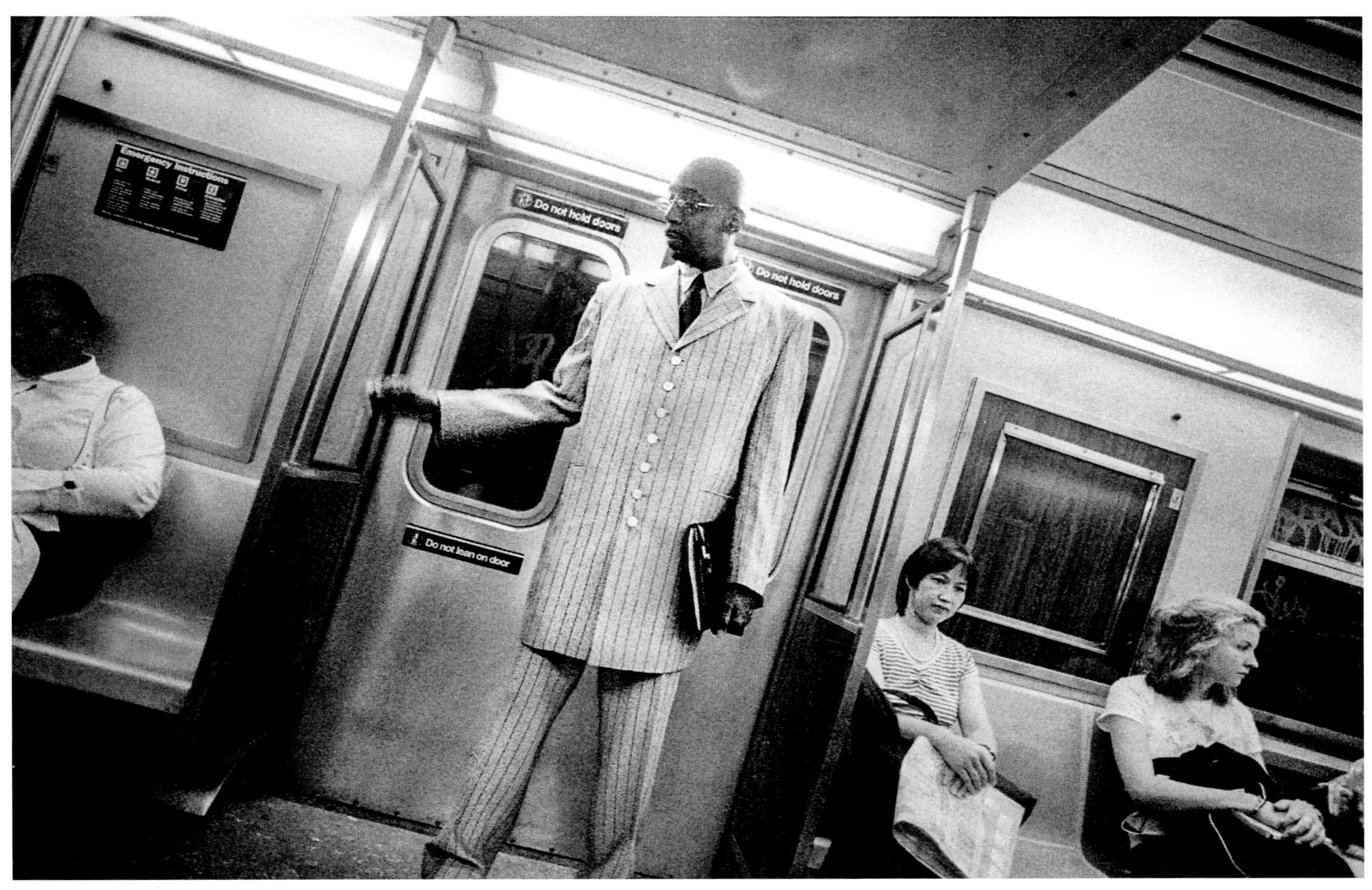
Emergency Instructions
Do not hold doors
Do not hold doors
Do not lean on door

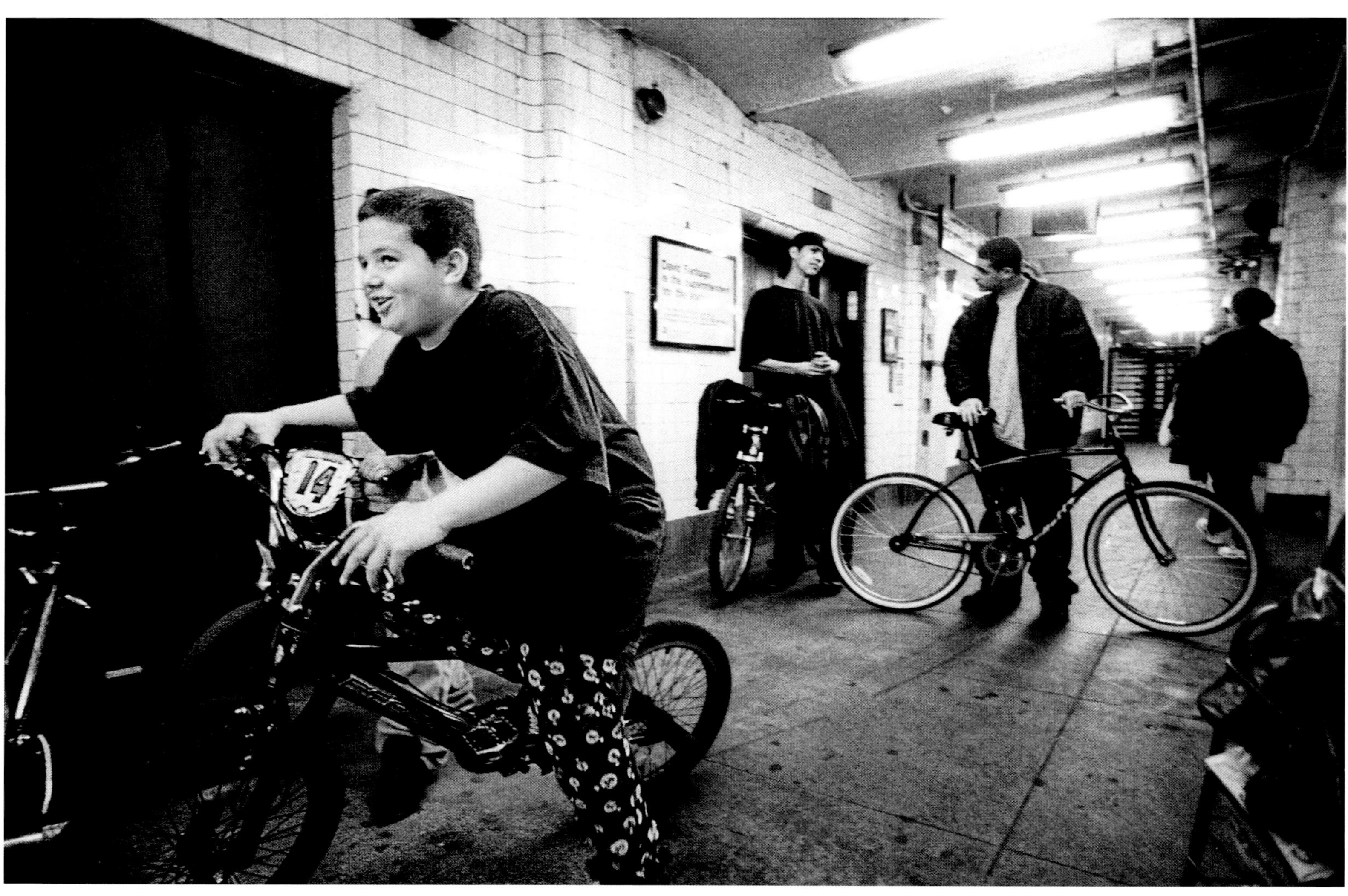

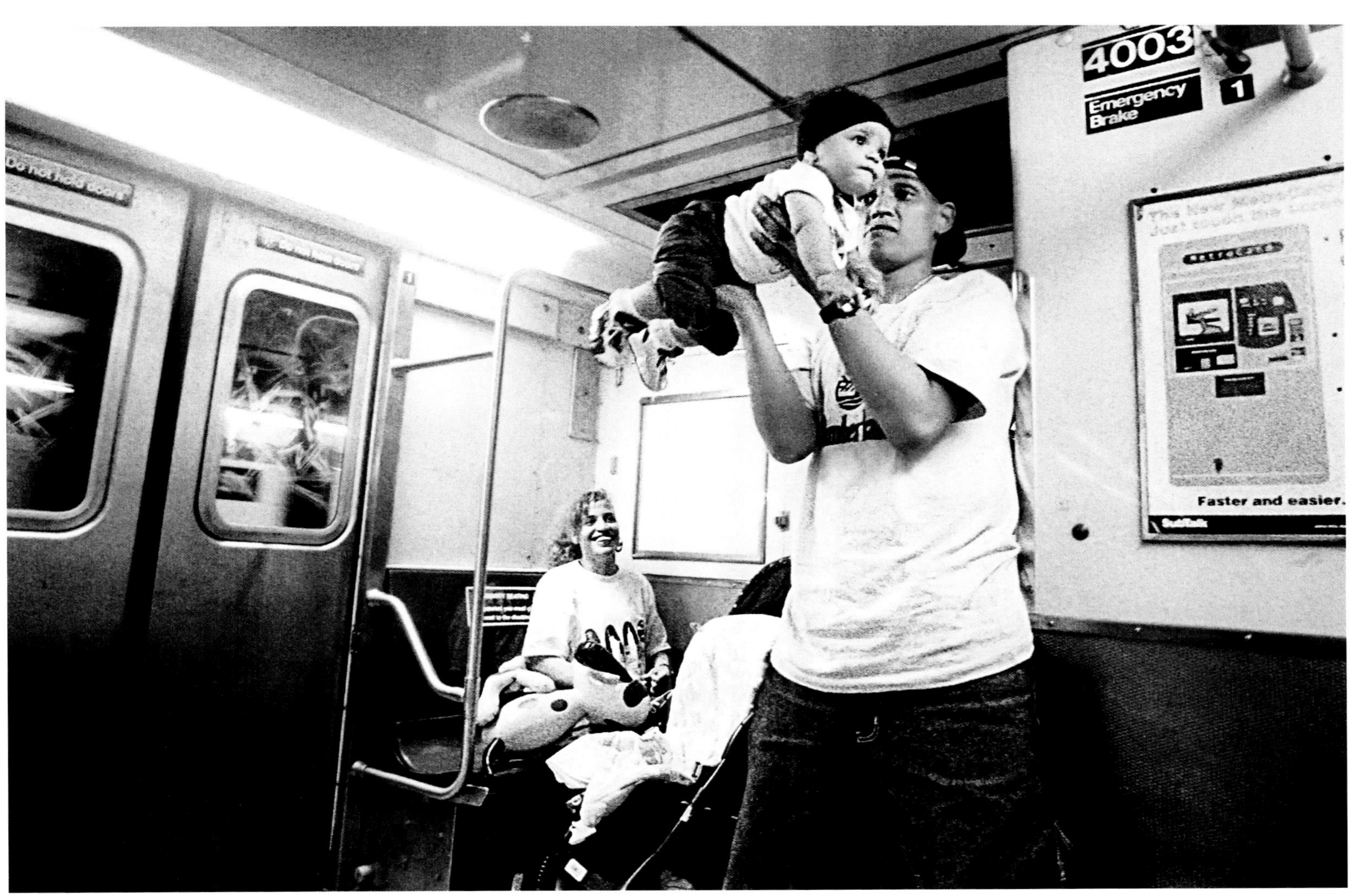
4003
Emergency
Brake
1
Faster and easier.

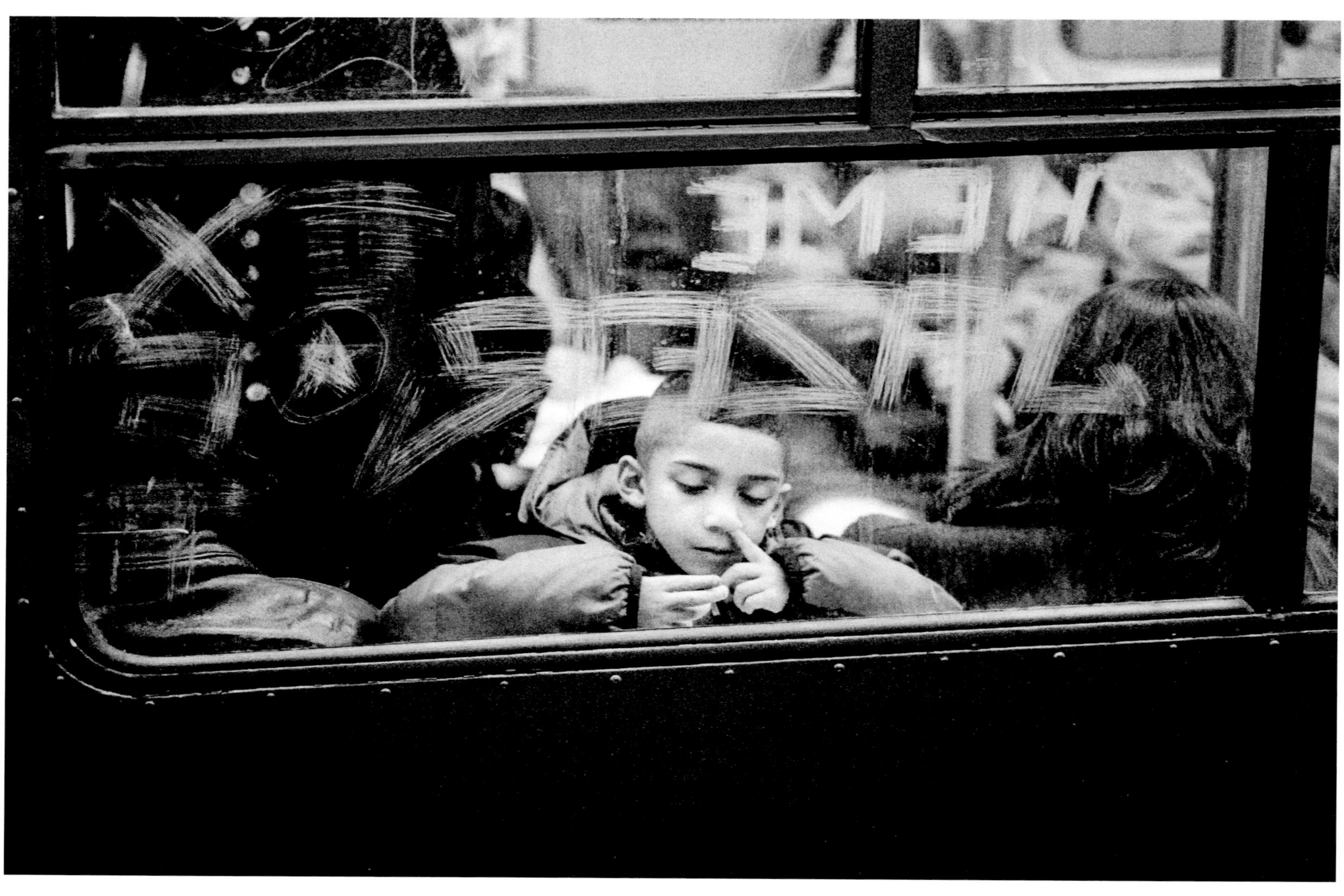

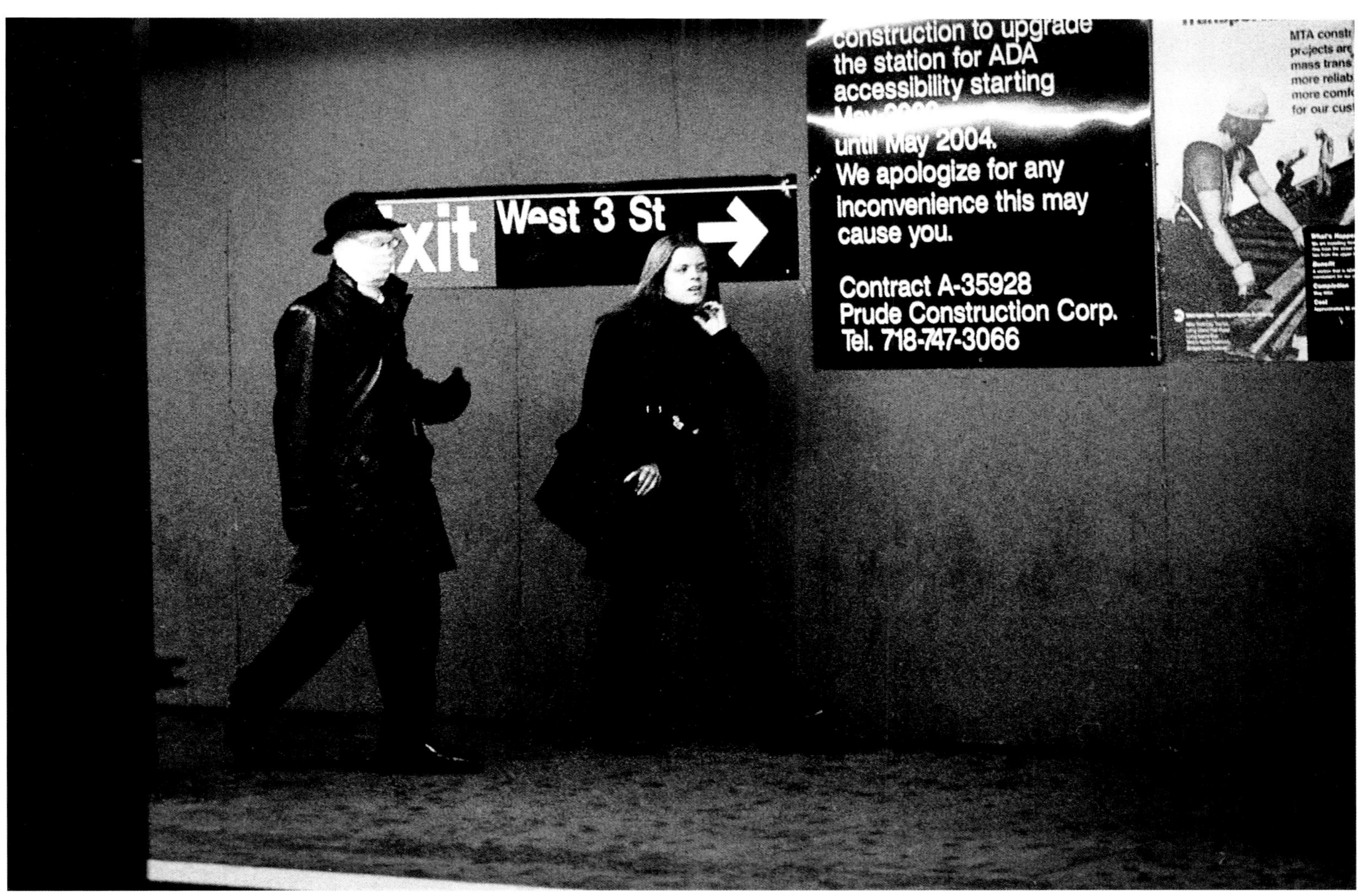
xit West 3 St →
construction to upgrade
the station for ADA
accessibility starting
May 2002
until May 2004.
We apologize for any
inconvenience this may
cause you.

Contract A-35928
Prude Construction Corp.
Tel. 718-747-3066
MTA constr
projects ar
mass trans
more reliab
more comfo
for our cust

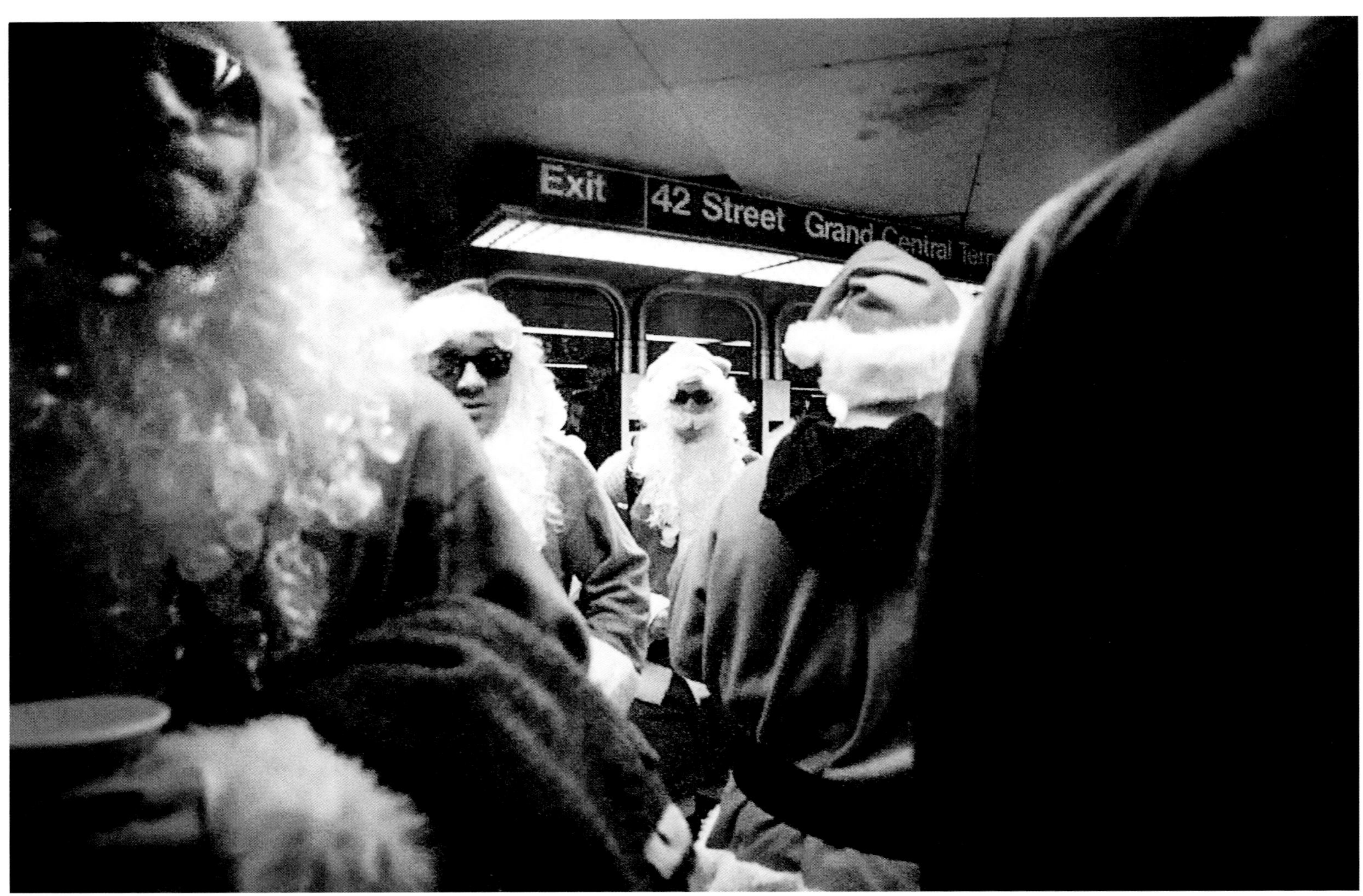

Exit 42 Street Grand Central Term

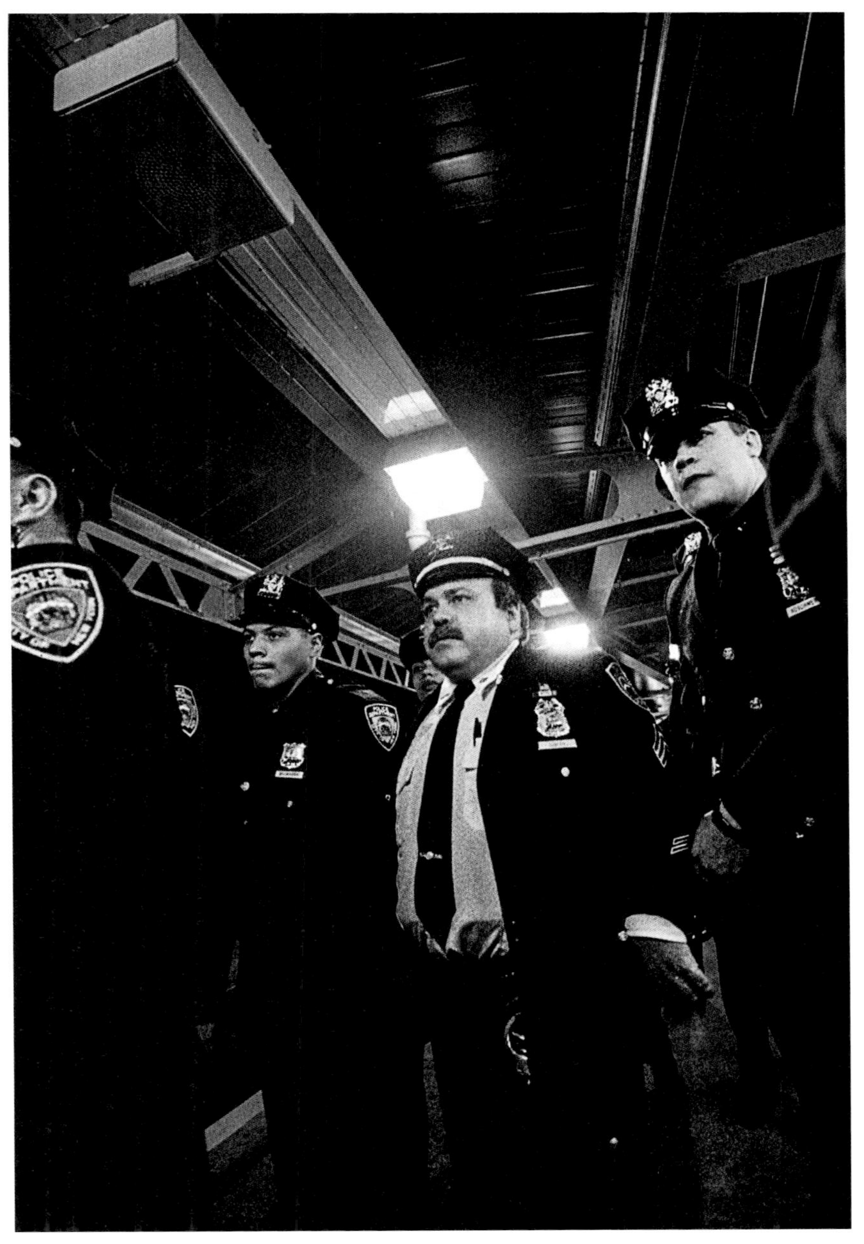

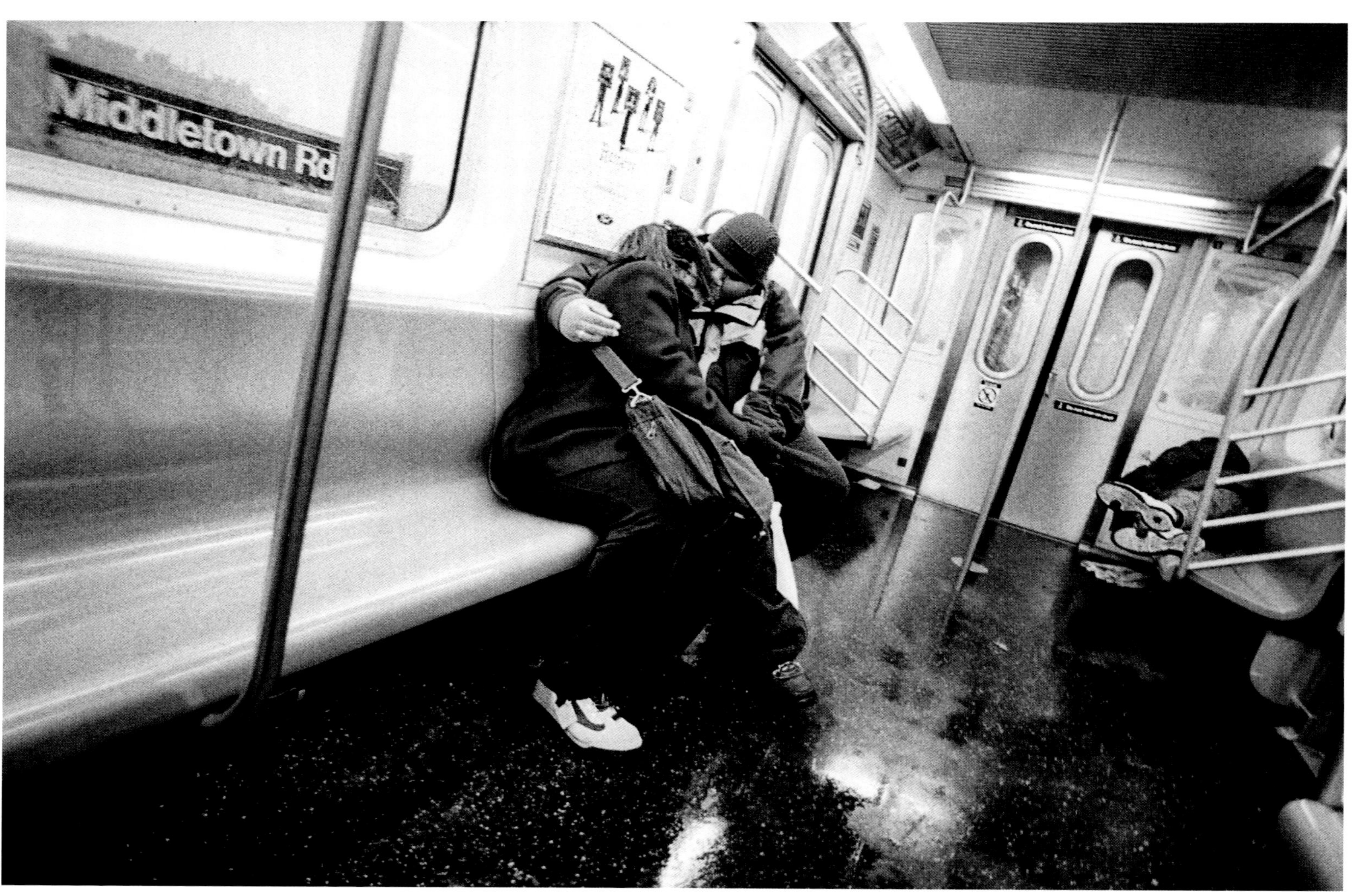

Middletown Rd

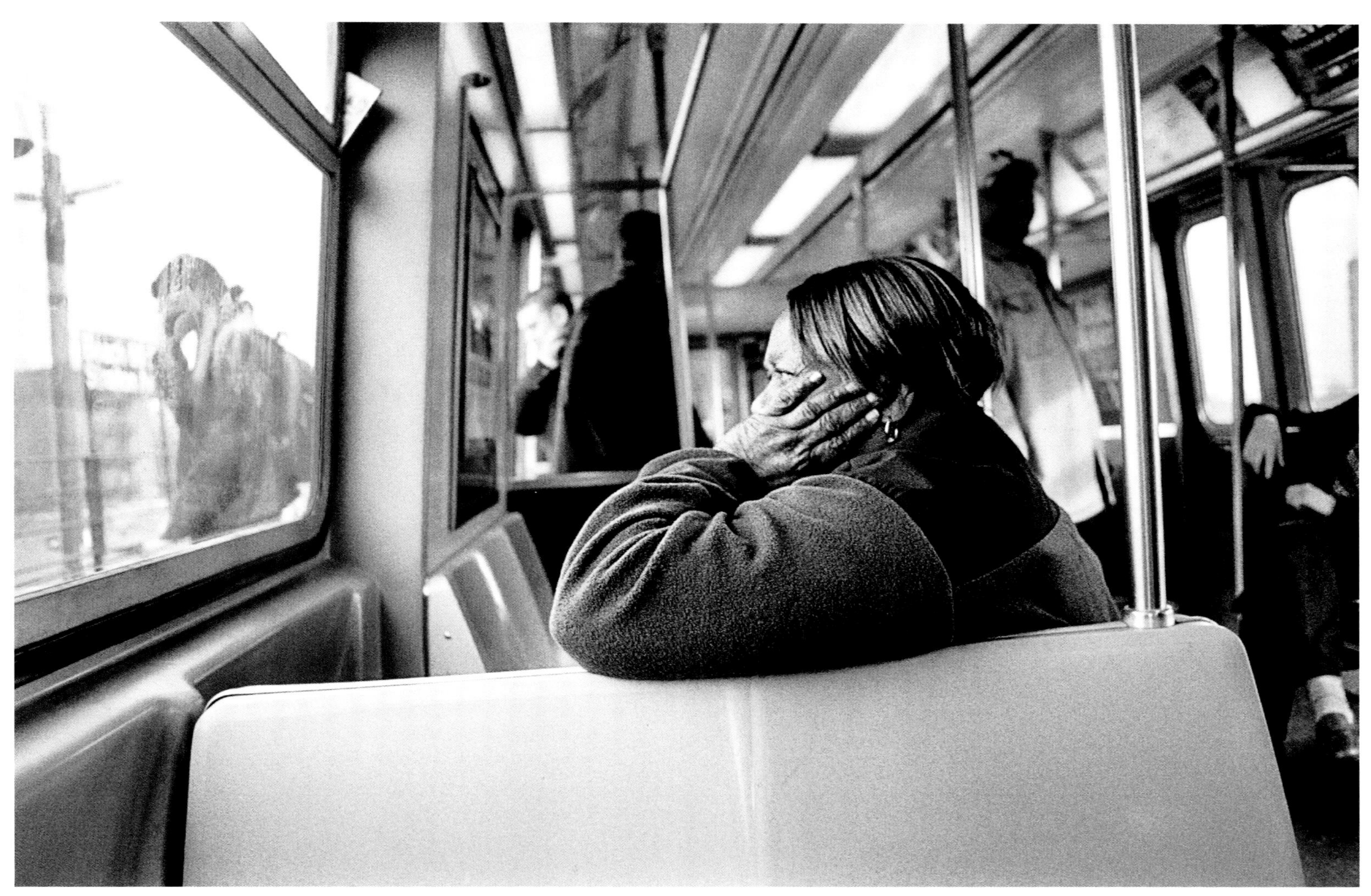

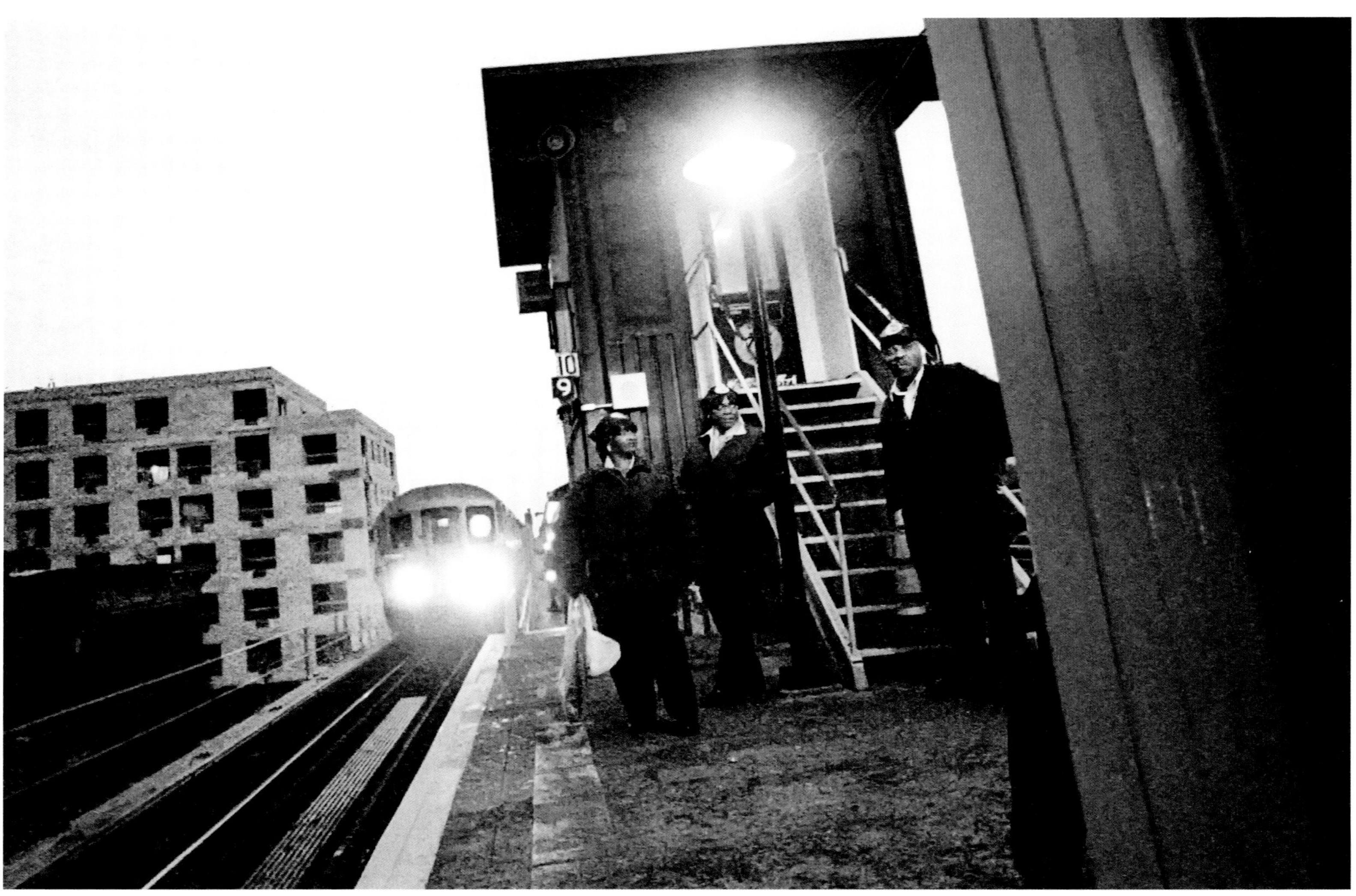

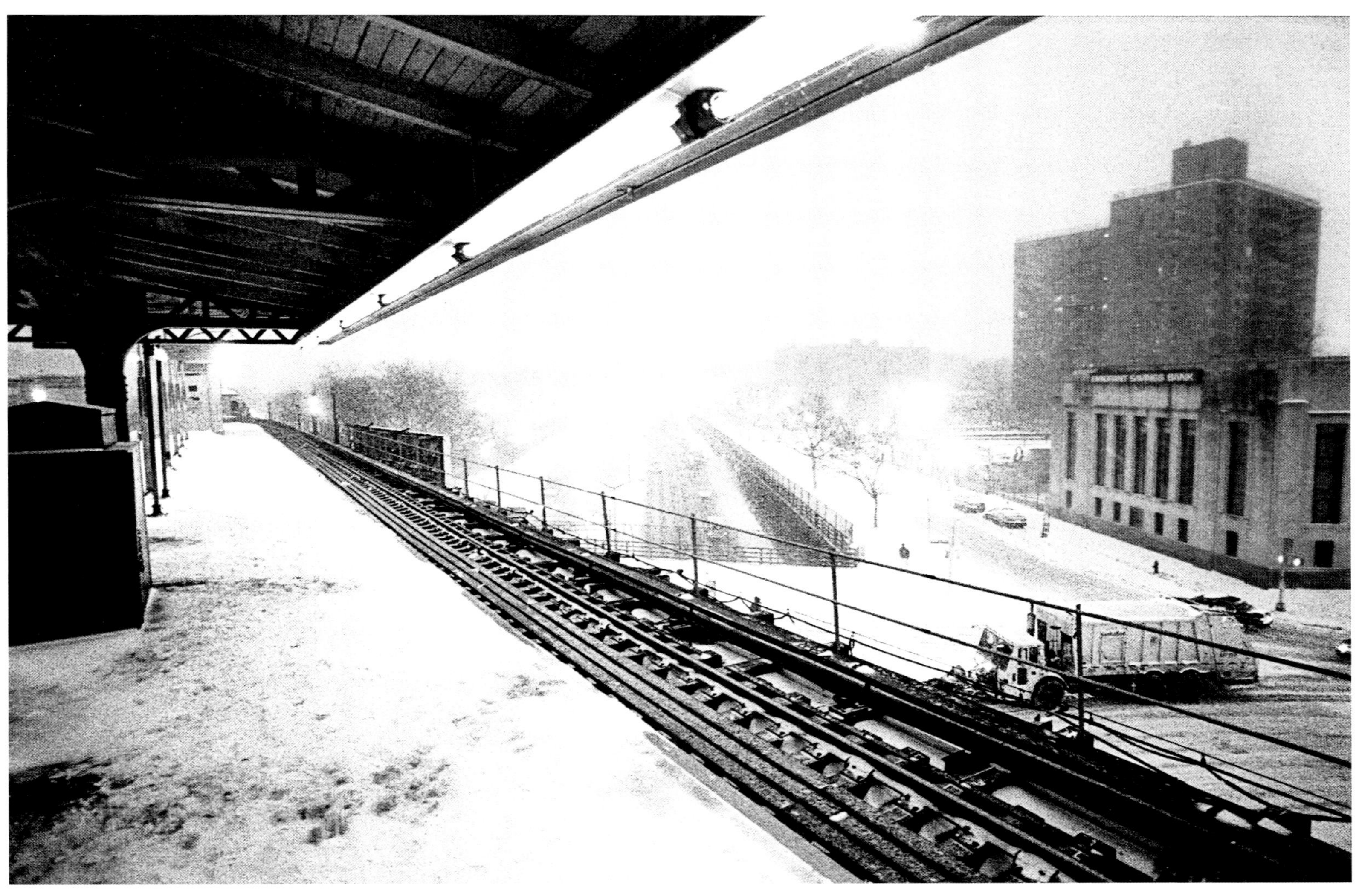

Coda

–Ed Hotchkiss

The project of creating this book has gone through many iterations. At first, I was simply focused on seeing film safely ensconced in its light-proof canister morph from negative to contact sheet to print. What would I find as I worked to make the image I remembered come to life? Could I successfully manipulate the exposure? What detail might I pick up on that I hadn't noticed before?

During many months of printing images, the perpetual night of the underground subway was replaced for me with the enforced night required by the darkroom. The stark, cinematic lighting of the subway emerged from trays filled with chemicals, bathed in the faint red hue of the darkroom safelight. The noises of the subway were far away, replaced now by jazz from my darkroom's speakers. At times I put my subway dreams aside to focus on photographing other topics, like my travels overseas. But consistently, over more than a decade, the subway lured me back and I built a portfolio of pictures.

As a photographer who does my own darkroom printing, I recognize that I have two distinct experiences with each image I make. There's the experience of taking the photograph, including technical considerations of shutter speed and f-stop, and artistic choices of composition and story. In the darkroom, my involvement with the picture becomes considerably more intimate yet controlled. I examine each millimeter of the negative to determine how best to express my vision on photographic paper. I decide whether the contrast, the exposure, and the development time say what I want about the picture.

When I began my odyssey, the only photographic option I had was the classic single-lens reflex camera, acetate film, and the darkroom. There were no cell-phone cameras with extreme low-light sensitivity, nor sophisticated software to enhance the images. However, I feel my black-and-white renditions convey the grit and graphics of the subway, as well as ennoble the riders. Eventually I realized that the photos themselves are more than shots of fleeting moments and constitute a document of the visual vernacular of a lost time.

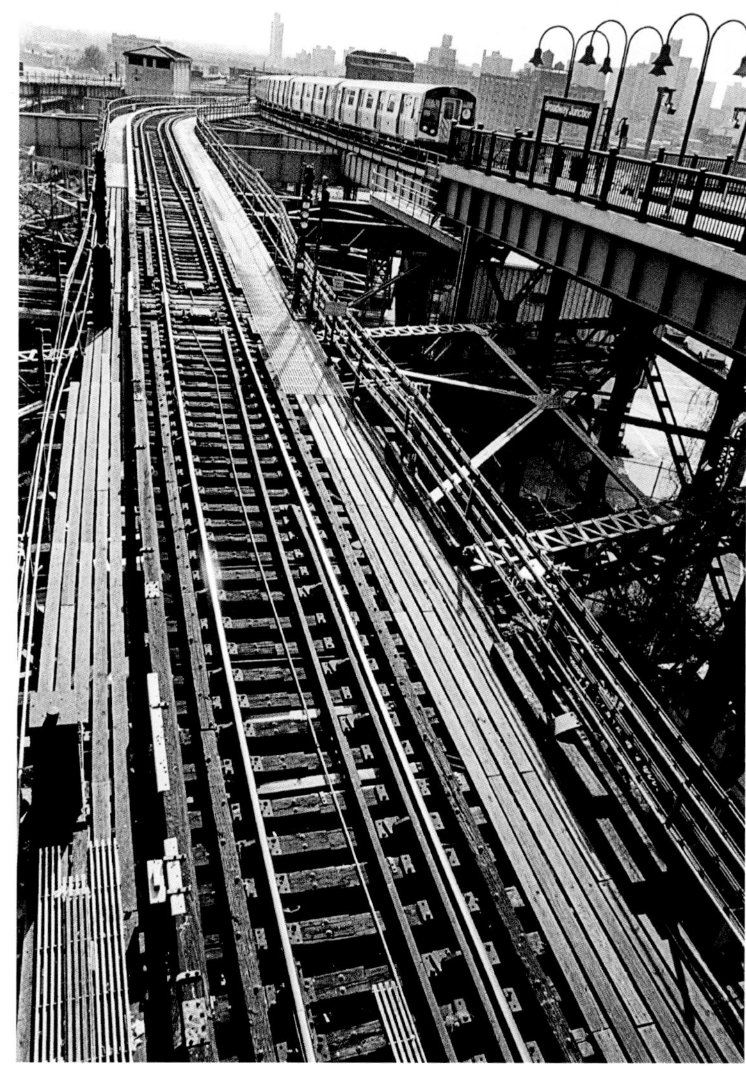
Broadway Junction

Afterword

–Lawrence Weschler

Ed Hotchkiss was born in Denver but did not stay put for long. Wanting to discover America beyond his home state, by age 21 he'd hitchhiked through all forty-eight states in the mainland United States. Currently, he has set his sights on going to every country in the world. He has been to over one hundred countries so far, though he still hopes to have visited them all before he hangs up his backpack for good. Ed plans not just to visit but to take the time to get a deep sense of each. And you can follow his ongoing adventures and ever-widening insights in that regard on his blog at his exploringed.com website.

But during the 1990s through the aughts, Ed's attention was focused on capturing the essence of the New York City subway. The point here, in our present context, is that with Ed Hotchkiss we have a world traveler who for the better part of his adult life has been based in and around the planet's greatest and most teeming city: New York. When he travels the world, to judge from his photo logs, he delights in landscape, but what he really loves doing is watching people everywhere and in all their profuse and dazzlingly various specificity. (He'd likely agree with Auden: "To me Art's subject is the human clay, / And landscape but a background to a torso; / All Cezanne's apples I would give away / For one small Goya or a Daumier.") And New York, for its part, is itself made up, precisely and maybe more so than any other city in the world, of people from all over the planet. This, too, is pertinent, for Ed's interest in people has never been solely individual: he has always been interested in the dance between people and groups of people and groups of groups. In how places work. And what better place to observe such interactions, usually playing out almost unconsciously and unawares, than down there in the subway?

"People talk about the United States as a melting pot," Ed tells me, "but that's not really the case. In New York, anyway, it's more of a parfait, this profusion of specific national communities, many concentrated in specific local neighborhoods—Guyanese in Ozone Park, Russians in Brighton Beach, Koreans in Flushing." He figures that each of the city's five boroughs is in fact made up of approximately fifteen different neighborhoods. And he has visited every one. "But in the subway, which is how I get to them all," he goes on, "it really is a melting pot—the entire world in microcosm, all the communities tumbling and scrambling all over one another, as, by and large peaceably, they just keep going about their days. And getting to observe that in turn is one of the things that keeps drawing me down there."

Or not so much that, exactly—like everybody else, trying to get from one place to another in the most efficient and affordable way, if not necessarily the most blithe and comfortable, is what draws us all down there. But most folks, as he notes, downshift into a sort of stupefied autopilot the moment they ford the subway turnstiles: resolutely ear-podded or eye-focused on their book or paper or magazine, or just plain trance-exhausted, they make a point, by and large, of not looking at each other. Ed, on the other hand, just can't stop looking—looking and seeing!

In his charming and vigorous reflections, he elucidates his method: how, in short, he managed to capture such a remarkably affecting sequence of moments, brimming as they are with such a generously sly and wryly pitched fellow feeling. Henri Cartier-Bresson, arguably one of the greatest street photographers of the last century, famously liked to speak of "the decisive moment," but Ed makes it clear that as far as his own practice has been concerned, it's always been more a question of steadying his gaze toward the ripening occasion. He snaps thousands of photos down there, but the real adventure, he'll be the first to admit, comes when he returns from down under to his home where he quickly dives into that other tunnel, his darkroom, developing the negatives and poring over the proof sheets, studying and assessing as has been his lifelong wont, panning for epiphanic gold.

"We live our lives," Sartre once observed, "as if we are telling ourselves a story, and we live surrounded by the stories of others." At the end of the day, Ed Hotchkiss is a master at evoking the bracing crisscross of tales that comprises the churning lifeworld of the underground city.

Lawrence Weschler, the award-winning veteran of the *New Yorker*, the *Atlantic*, the *New York Times Magazine*, *McSweeney's*, and the *Believer*, is the author of over twenty books of narrative nonfiction, including *Seeing Is Forgetting the Name of the Thing One Sees* (on artist Robert Irwin), *True to Life* (on David Hockney), *Vermeer in Bosnia*, and most recently, *And How Are You, Dr. Sacks?* (a biographical memoir of his thirty-five-year friendship with the neurologist Oliver Sacks). For more, see his website at www.lawrenceweschler.com.

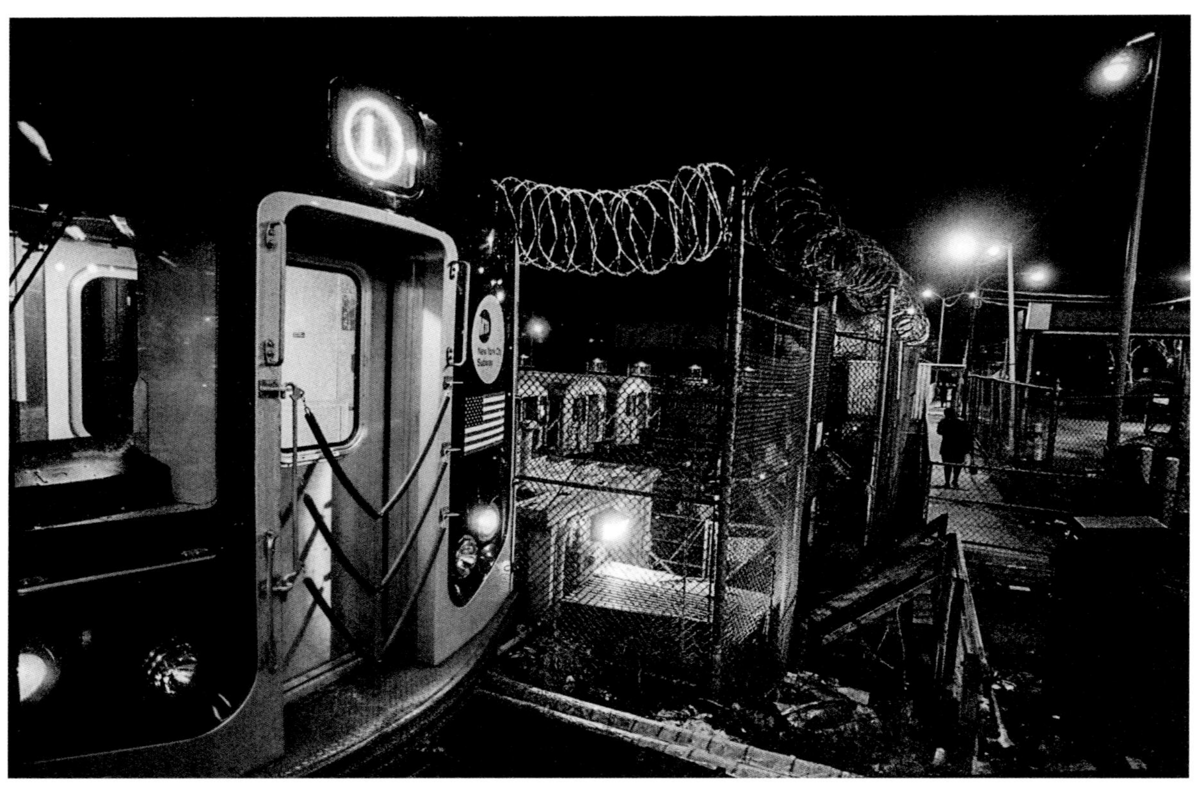

Acknowledgments

Many friends, too many to mention all, provided comments on the photos; in particular, Peter Goldschmidt for years provided invaluable help in the ultimate selection. My daughter Ayan has been a pivotal and constant component of the post-production process through its multiple stages. She did an incredible job editing the text and photos with an important contribution from Caitlin Goldschmidt. Harvey Stein, a great photographer with many published books under his belt, provided important insight on the photobook business. I greatly appreciate Alberto Sandoval's feedback on the design during the process of creating initial layouts of the book. Stephen Sherman, with perfectionist execution, enhanced my negatives into the final images and prints. Blossom Nicinski provided critical input for my essay of this experience. Robin Whalley of Lenscraft Photography patiently instructed me on how to scan my negatives into high-resolution digital files. I am grateful that the talented Lawrence Weschler found the time to write the afterword. My wife, Khadija, has been unbelievably supportive in my obsession to document the New York City subway, where I have spent hundreds of hours and taken thousands of pictures. However, this book would not be possible without all the people in the images, none of whom I met but all of whom I feel I know in some way.

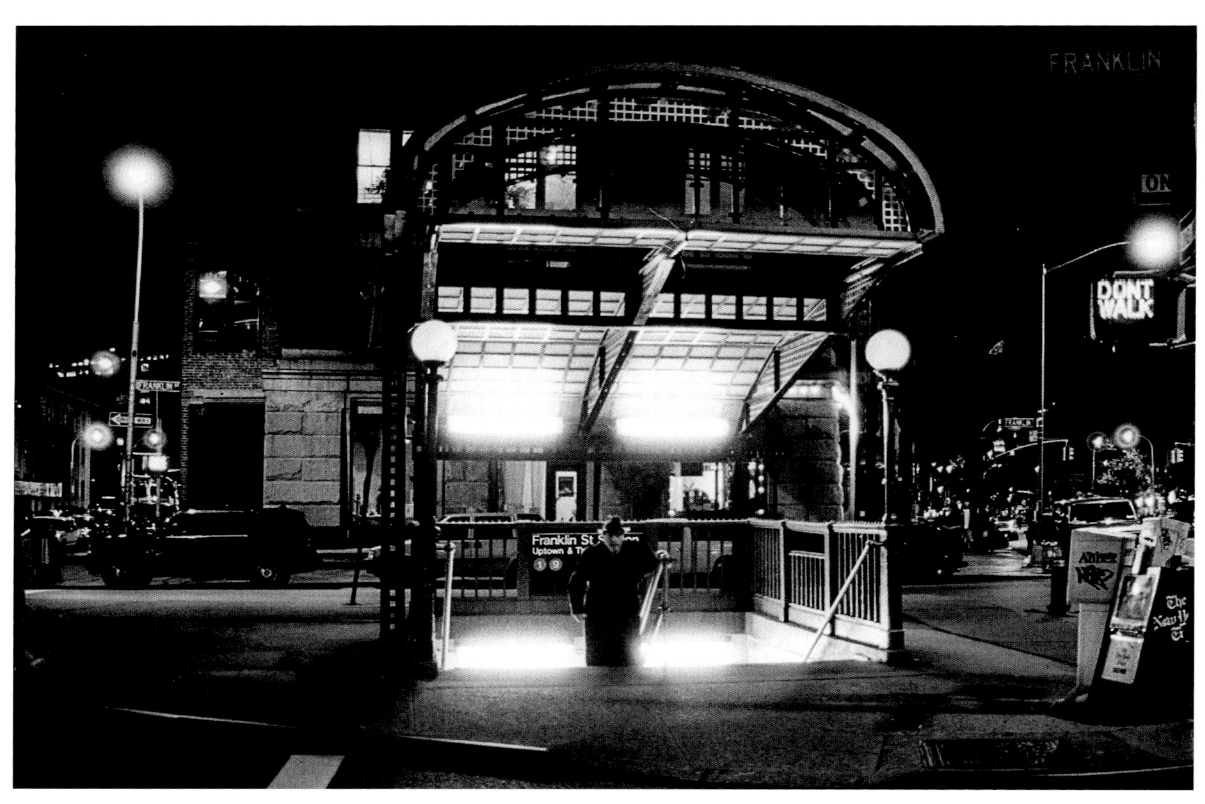
FRANKLIN
DON'T WALK
Franklin St Station
Uptown & Tr
The New York Times

Ed Hotchkiss is a New York City–based photographer and the founder of www.ExploringEd.com, where he blogs about travel and photography. He has traveled to six continents, over one hundred countries, and every US state. He specializes in photographing street life, urban locales, musical events, natural landscapes, waterfalls, and night scenes. His mission is to travel to every country in the world and to keep exploring the neighborhoods of New York City. He can be followed @ExploringEdTravel on Instagram, Facebook, and Pinterest.

Plates

Page	Title	Date	Train Lines	Station / Train	Borough
1	Train and Tracks in Snow	January 2005	6	Pelham Parkway	Bronx
5	Six People Sitting in Subway Car	April 2004	J	Manhattan train	Queens
6	Underground Sunlight	February 2004	3	Downtown train	Manhattan
11	Atlantic Avenue Meeting	April 2000	D,Q	Atlantic Avenue	Brooklyn
12	Couple under Ad with Baby	October 2000	4	Downtown train	Manhattan
13	Mariachi Musician with Large Guitar	March 2004	1	Downtown train	Manhattan
14	Doors Opening at Union Square	February 2001	5	Union Square	Manhattan
15	Woman in Braids with Two Children	July 2000	4,5	Downtown train	Manhattan
16	Conductor and Platform Cameras	February 2001	4,5	Union Square	Manhattan
17	Man in Fedora	April 2004	J,Z	Jamaica Center	Queens
18	Broadway Junction Escalator	April 2004	A,C,J,L,Z	Broadway Junction	Brooklyn
21	Men with Newspaper, Book, and Bicycle	May 2000	4,5	Downtown train	Manhattan
22	Woman in Christopher Street Station	October 2001	1,9	Christopher Street	Manhattan
23	Fashionably Dressed Party	December 2003	S	Times Square	Manhattan
24	Newspaper Stand	April 2004	E,J,Z	Jamaica Center	Queens
25	Token Booth	March 2004	2,3,4,5,D,Q	Atlantic Avenue	Brooklyn
27	Woman Leaning on Column	August 2000	4	Grand Central	Manhattan
28	Two Men in Suits Sitting Tightly Together	May 2000	4,5	Downtown train	Manhattan
30	Six People on Platform Bench	March 2004	A,C,E	Port Authority	Manhattan
31	42nd Street Turnstiles	February 2001	1,2,3,9	Times Square	Manhattan
32	Boy Dribbling Basketball	February 2004	A,C	168th Street	Manhattan
33	Person with Briefcase on Lower Platform	February 2004	A	181st Street	Manhattan
34	Two Women on Platform, One on Steps	September 2004	1,2,3,9	Times Square	Manhattan
35	Woman and Dancing Boys	December 2003	S	Times Square	Manhattan
36	Legion of Mary	March 2000	4,5,6,7	Grand Central	Manhattan
38	Man in Suit and White Socks	April 2000	F	Manhattan train	Brooklyn
39	Man and Teenagers in NY Yankees Caps	February 2001	1,2,3,7,9,S	Times Square	Manhattan
40	Couple on Coney Island Train	January 2005	Q	Downtown train	Manhattan
42	Man in Black Leather	October 2000	4,5	Uptown train	Manhattan
43	Man with Flipped Tie and Children	May 2000	4,5	Downtown train	Manhattan
45	Woman and Shopping Cart	December 2004	6	Downtown train	Manhattan
47	Father Holding Baby	October 2009	A	Columbus Circle	Manhattan
48	Woman in Waiting Area	December 2004	6	Uptown train	Manhattan
51	Masked Man and Policeman	October 2001	1,9	Christopher Street	Manhattan
52	MTA Worker Cleaning Platform	January 2004	1,9	66th Street	Manhattan
53	Policewoman with Baton	October 2001	1,9	Christopher Street	Manhattan
54	Man in Wheelchair on Platform	April 2000	6	Grand Central	Manhattan

Page	Title	Date	Train Lines	Station / Train	Borough
55	Woman and Sleeping Children	August 2001	4	Downtown train	Manhattan
57	Woman with Children at Broadway Junction	May 2011	L	Broadway Junction	Brooklyn
58	A Cappella Singers	March 1996	7	Times Square	Manhattan
60	Flying Break Dancer	October 2001	1,2,3,9	Times Square	Manhattan
61	Break Dancer on Head	October 2001	1,2,3,9	Times Square	Manhattan
62	Couple By Stair Railing	February 2001	1,2,3,9	Times Square	Manhattan
63	Four Young Men with Baggy Clothes	October 2001	1,2,3,9	Times Square	Manhattan
65	Woman Reading Magazine	February 2001	6	Uptown train	Manhattan
66	Jesus Leaving Train	October 2006	A,C,E	West 4th Street	Manhattan
68	Elderly Man in Suit	March 2000	1,2,3,9	Times Square	Manhattan
69	Woman in Wimple	February 2001	4,5,6,7	Grand Central	Manhattan
71	Man Surrounded by Faces in Car	October 2009	A	Columbus Circle	Manhattan
72	Two Women in Dresses, Two Men in Jackets	October 2009	A,C,E	West 4th Street	Manhattan
73	Woman with Cross at Turnstile	October 2002	A,B,C,D,E,F,Q,V	West 4th Street	Manhattan
74	Young Man with Skateboard	May 2011	N	Queens train	Queens
75	Young Lady with Roller Blades	November 2009	4	Bronx train	Bronx
76	Witch and Warlock	October 2000	S	Times Square	Manhattan
77	Two Couples and Woman Kicking Leg	December 2003	1,2,3,9	Times Square	Manhattan
79	Woman Reading with Child	March 2004	1	Downtown train	Manhattan
81	Bald Man Sitting on Platform Floor	October 2009	N,R,Q,W	Times Square	Manhattan
82	Man with Guitar in Subway Car	August 2001	4,5	Downtown train	Manhattan
83	Man Eating on Platform Bench	December 2002	4,5,6	Grand Central	Manhattan
85	Tall Man with Long Suit Coat	August 2004	A	Downtown train	Manhattan
86	Boys with Bicycles by Elevators	February 2004	A	181st Street	Manhattan
87	Flying Baby	May 2000	A	Downtown train	Manhattan
88	Boy Looking Out of Scratched Window	February 2001	7	Times Square	Manhattan
91	Invisible Man	October 2002	A,C,E	West 4th Street	Manhattan
92	Santas with Sunglasses	December 2008	4,5,6,7	Grand Central	Manhattan
93	Police at Yankee Stadium Station	October 2000	4,B,D	Yankee Stadium	Bronx
94	Couple and Sleeping Person	January 2005	6	Middletown Road	Bronx
95	Woman Looking Out Car Window	November 2009	A	Beach 60th Street	Queens
96	Three MTA Workers on Platform	November 2009	3	New Lots Avenue	Brooklyn
99	Parkchester Station in Snow	January 2005	6	Parkchester	Bronx
102	Train Approaching Broadway Junction	November 2009	L	Broadway Junction	Brooklyn
106	L Train at Canarsie Yard	April 2004	L	Canarsie	Brooklyn
108	Man Exiting Franklin Street Station	April 1998	1,9	Franklin Street	Manhattan
112	East New York Subway Car Yard	November 2009	L	Manhattan train	Brooklyn

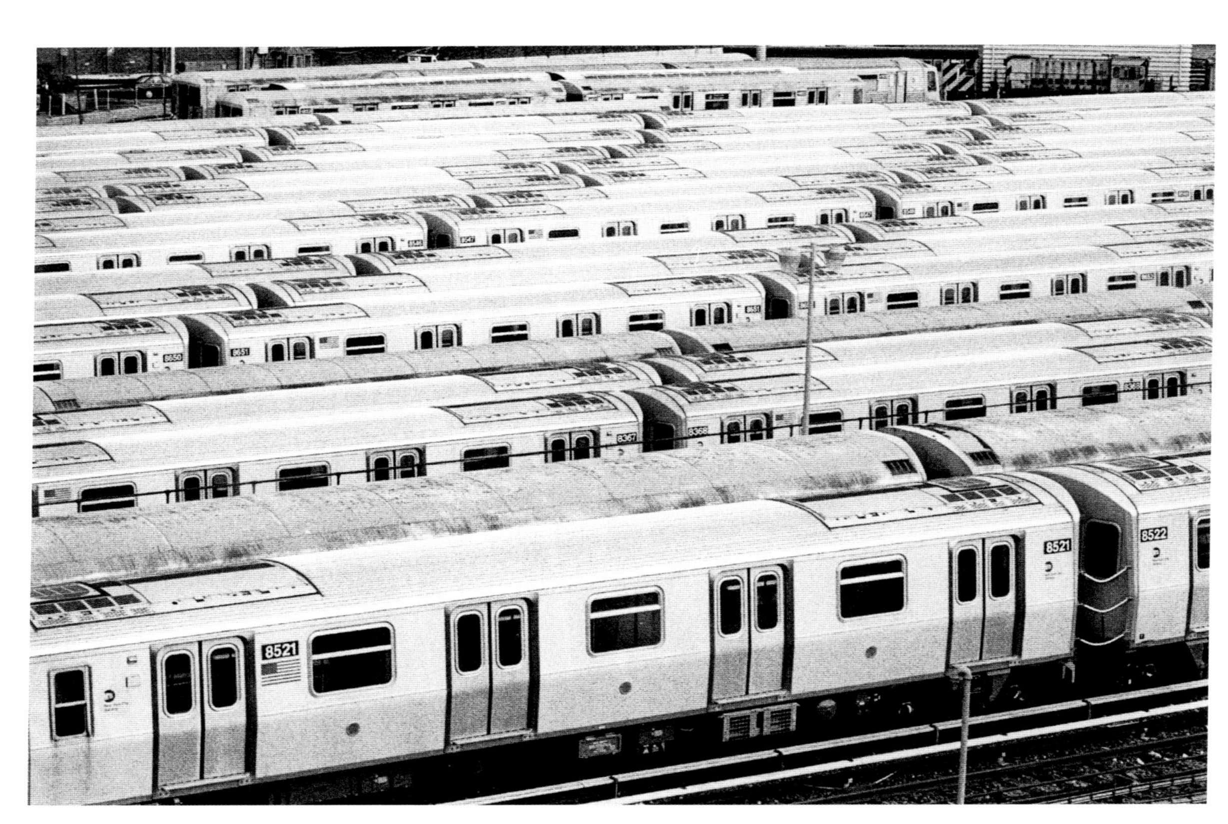